Rivers from

Eden

Forty days of intimate conversation with God

✠

Eden and Brad Jersak

RIVERS FROM EDEN

Forty Days of Intimate Conversation with God

✠

EDEN AND BRAD JERSAK

FRESH WIND PRESS

©2004 Fresh Wind Press

Written by Eden and Brad Jersak

This publication may almost always be reproduced and transmitted in any way you can imagine. You only need to ask. We usually say yes.

Cover design by Brad Jersak at Fresh Wind Press

Printed in Altona, Manitoba, CANADA by D.W. Friesen and Sons Ltd. Second Printing.

National Library of Canada Cataloguing in Publication

Jersak, Brad, 1964- , Jersak Eden, 1963-
    Rivers from Eden: Forty Days of Intimate Conversation with God / Brad Jersak and Eden Jersak

ISBN 0-9733586-3-7

    1. Spirituality life--Christianity. 2. Prayer--Christianity. 3. Listening--Religious aspects--Christianity. I. Jersak, Brad, 1964- , Jersak, Eden, 1963- II. Title.

Fresh Wind Press
2170 Maywood Court
Abbotsford, BC V2S 4Z1
www.freshwindpress.com

contents

how to use this book

The purpose of this book is to help you make listening prayer a lifestyle by modelling an approach to prayer through which your time with God can become an intimate and interactive meeting.

Our premise, described in detail in *Can You Hear Me? Tuning In to the God Who Speaks,* is that all of God's children can learn to hear his voice (Job 33:14; John 10:27) and see his face (Hebrews 12:2; 2 Corinthians 4:6). When the ears and eyes of your heart are opened, prayer becomes more than a mere religious exercise. It is a real meeting with a Living Friend.

Your heart is God's temple or home, a place designed specifically for meeting with him. After reading each day's question, settle down to ask the Lord where he would like to meet with you. He may present you with a visual scene, like the Garden of Eden, the green pastures of Psalm 23 or the throne room of heaven. Take time to behold him and to worship him in that place. Then ask him the question of the day. What comes to mind? Watch what God does—listen to what he says. Afterwards, you might want to journal the conversation, weighing carefully what you've seen and heard. This will also help the message sink deeper into your heart.

If doubt accuses you of making up answers, why not try to actually do that? First, come up with your own answer to the question, and then give God his turn. Take note of the contrast in the quality of the answers.

Apart from aiding your own listening prayer times, we hope these questions will fulfill two other specific needs:

1. After attending several listening prayer seminars and reading *Can You Hear Me?,* some folks have confessed that even though they have tasted the joy of listening prayer, they have yet to make it a lifestyle. They realize that asking questions is a major key to hearing God, but they need a primer to get them started.

Thus, we have selected forty questions that God answers regularly, many of which can be asked repeatedly. Our hope is that by the fortieth day, two-way prayer will have become your favorite habit. No doubt you will also develop many of your own questions by then.

2. The questions in this book also reflect the need for listening prayer to move from private faith to public faith—from the prayer closet to the street. This spiritual "respiration"—inhaling the life of God in personal reflection and exhaling the mercy of God into the world he loves—recalls the spirituality of Jesus in the Beatitudes (Matthew 5:3-11). Approaching prayer in this fashion will guard your heart against an addiction to navel gazing, focusing on self rather than God or others.

Having said all that, it's time to introduce you to my wife and best friend, Eden Jersak.

íntroducíng eden

This book came like an unexpected child. Just like Abraham's wife Sarah, I laughed when Brad suggested I write a book with him. But now here we are, about to give birth and eagerly anticipating what lies ahead. While working on this book, I have experienced many of the same emotions, aches, and pains I did carrying each of our three boys. Some days were euphoric as I felt the movement of what was growing inside me. Other days, I grappled with fear of the unknown—can I really do this? As the weight of what I was discovering with my God became heavier, my spiritual muscles ached with the stretching of that growth. But now I'm nearly full-term, waiting only for the labor to begin and looking forward to seeing what has been formed.

I hope that reading through my journey will encourage you in your own relationship with God. But don't be satisfied with what I hear from God. Run to God and ask him these questions yourself. I'm confident that when you call on God, he will answer, just as he does for me. Sometimes his reply will come as a thought, sometimes merely as a sensation, and some of you will see it in vivid colors. It doesn't matter how you see or hear God. The most important thing is to open the eyes and ears of your heart and wait in eager expectation for God to respond to your queries.

As you embark on this journey, seek out a place where you are comfortable, somewhere the world won't be clamoring quite so loudly for your attention. When you find that sweet spot, go there as often as possible. Ask Jesus to join you there or to take you to some place in your heart that will be your meeting place.

You will find that I have many meeting places with Jesus. Some are personal favorites because of what Jesus has said to me there. Others are places I've been to in this world but can also go to in my heart. Some are completely new and absolutely full of wonder for me, places that have been created specifically for my meetings with Jesus. There is no limit to where he is willing to meet with you and no limit to where you and Jesus can go from there.

I have a question for Jesus as we embark: "Jesus, what do you want the readers of this book to know?"

I want them to know that I dwell in their hearts and that I long to walk through this journey with them. I have secrets and stories to share with them there. I'm inviting them to walk with me and talk with me.

a River flowed
from eden
watering
the garden...

✠

genesis 2:10

Day 1

✠

God, who are you?

Who is God to you? Our spiritual journey begins with this question, because, above all else, we need to know God.

A friend of mine was struggling with life, on a steady decline into despair. Each night she prayed, "God, please fix me or kill me!" One day, things took a discernable turn for the better. Rather than merely surviving, she began to overcome. When I asked her to account for the change, she replied, "I stopped asking God to fix me and began to ask, 'Who are you?' instead."

Contrary to popular belief, we don't get to fashion God according to our personal wants or whims. Only God can reveal himself to us. This revelation, far from being coldly theological, is always relational and seasonal. As you ask, "Who are you?" God will answer according to your current need: "I am your _____."

Herein, you'll see Eden relating to both God the Father and to Jesus Christ according to the needs of her heart. How about you? What aspect of God's personhood is he showing you these days? Ask him why. And consider this: What if what God is telling you is true? What does that mean for your life? How will today be different?

God, who are you?

I've come to meet Jesus at a small patch of green grass in my heart's yard. Together, we sit on a comfortable swinging seat that is shaded from the blazing sun. My question for him today and, ultimately, his answer, will be the grid through which I live this life.

"Who are you?" The rhythm of the swing doesn't miss a beat.

I'm your Redeemer.

I smile, because I know it's true! I've been aware of his redemptive power for a long, long time. But his answer begs me to ask more questions.

"How is it that you are able to take all of my sin, other people's sins against me, my bad decisions, poor judgment, and all the other ways I fail you and then redeem it? The way I see it, I keep giving you garbage and you keep producing fruit. How is this possible?"

Jesus takes a deep breath, not out of exasperation but as if he's been waiting with some anticipation to answer this question.

I love taking what the enemy uses as tools to kill and destroy, and turning it into life.

I turn to look fully in his eyes, and when I do, I see the spark that has been ignited behind them. He really does enjoy his role as Redeemer.

Can I ask *you* a question, Eden?

"Okay!"

14

What difference does my redemption make in your life?

I realize that he has just called me to worship. My heart leaps at the opportunity.

"For years, I spent much of my time and energy looking back at my sin, always looking for something I had missed or afraid that my pleas for mercy were somehow inadequate. I moved forward in my journey but with halting, uncertain steps. When I discovered your glorious power to redeem, my life changed. My sin was no longer a reason to stop the journey; it no longer had the power to wound my heart and cripple my legs.

"Your ability to redeem me from guilt and shame propels me forward on the journey. You have taken me to some amazing places through your redemption. Some of the places we've walked together were only accessible because you were with me. I couldn't go there alone. Your redemption also leaves a sweet fragrance behind. It draws me to follow you even closer. I can see my journey has always been at your expense. Thank you!

"The difference your redemption makes in my life? Easy: Now I have a life!"

He grabs my hand and sandwiches it between his.

I love the journey we're on. Please don't ever let the cost of it get in the way of where you want to go. I've paid for it gladly!

Day 2

✠

tell me what you are like

As God begins to reveal himself to us, we want to get an accurate sense of what he is like. For example, while God may reveal himself as Father or King or Lover, we might also want to say, "Yes, Lord, but tell me about your character. What type of person am I dealing with? How would you describe yourself? Some fathers are neglectful, some kings are tyrants, and some lovers are unfaithful. But tell me, what are you like?"

Mike, an Anglican priest, recently paraphrased Psalm 103 to me. He said, in passing, "Hey, Brad, the Lord wants you to know that he's gracious and compassionate. And he doesn't get angry very quickly." Sounds good to me.

Ask the Lord today what he is like. What is one aspect of his character—one descriptive word—that he would use to reveal himself to you? Ask him what that word means to him. And, once again, ask yourself what if this word is true? What will it mean in your life today?

tell me what
are you like

A million words swirl around my head like a gigantic tornado. I can't even catch one let alone choose only one to describe God.

Aren't you supposed to ask *me* what I'm like?

The tornado stops dead. Small pieces of paper drift to the ground as if it were snowing. They cover the ground completely around our feet. I look up into the eyes of my Heavenly Father with just a little embarrassment.

"Please, tell me what you're like!"

He tugs gently at my hand and we sit down, cross-legged, facing each other in the midst of all these little pieces of paper.

I'm like a lot of things. I could use any one of these words lying around us to describe myself. It does seem a bit overwhelming, doesn't it? But I'm glad you asked me, because there is one word I really want you to know me as: *attentive*.

I'm stunned. All of these words and that's the one he chooses? He is the God of the Universe, Maker of Heaven and Earth, King of Kings and Lord of Lords, and he describes himself as "attentive"?

"Are you sure you want to use *that* word?" I ask, rooting through the papers. "There must be more powerful words in this pile, more grand and exalted words. How about I give you another chance?"

I don't need another chance, Eden. That's the word I choose

to describe myself today.

"Then tell me more. Why do you choose 'attentive' to describe yourself?"

I choose it because it's true and because you need to know it. I *am* the God of the universe and all those other amazing things, but I'm also attentive to you! Do you—can you—believe that?

"I don't have a hard time believing you are attentive. I just don't understand why. With so many other people and things going on in this world, why would you be attentive to me?"

Because you matter to me! The things you do, the things you say, the desires of your heart, your pain, your joy—they all matter to me, and so I attend to you. I'm always listening for your voice and watching for your next success. I'm not attentive because I'm controlling; I'm attentive because I care. I pay attention to the details of your life, because I love you. How does that feel?

"Powerful."

I thought you might see it my way. You don't have to fight for my attention. This isn't some big cosmic contest to see who can grab my attention by being really good or super spiritual. I'm the God of the universe, and I care about my creation. I care enough to be attentive to all of the details—even yours!

"Does that mean that I'm not bothering you with the little stuff?"

That's right!

"That you're always thinking about me?"

Can't stop!

"That who I am really matters to you?"

Absolutely!

I want to throw my arms around him, but he beats me to it. As always, he knew exactly what I wanted!

Day 3

✠

show me what you are like

God is so committed to revealing who he is and what he is like that he continually makes use of objects and symbols to which he compares himself. Throughout Scripture, God tells us that he is like a lion, a rock, a whirlwind or any number of things. He uses a seemingly endless array of metaphors, from tiny flowers to consuming fire, identifying with familiar images in our world to show us his multi-faceted nature. These word pictures express much more than literary creativity. They are meant to touch our hearts at some point of need.

Today, ask the Lord to bring to mind one object or symbol that represents him. Ask him why he is like that object or symbol. Then ask him how this object or symbol relates to you. If God is truly like that, what does that do for your heart? What does that mean for your faith journey? What does that mean for you today? Remember, don't try to figure it out on your own—ask him!

show me what you are like

The depths of my heart need the answer to this question today.

"Would you please peel away all of my 'Sunday school' answers and open my eyes to see you for who you really are?

I am your Anchor.

"Wow, I guess I was expecting more, or at least not such a common answer. Why an anchor?"

Look at it, Eden. See its size and strength compared to your boat? You will never need to worry that your anchor won't hold! It is more than enough to handle the storms you've endured and the storms that are yet to come.

I take those words to heart as my mind flashes back to recent events, times when the boat that represents my life strained against that Anchor.

"Does that anchor restrict me?"

The restrictions are mine. I tied myself to you willingly when I died for you. I won't let go; I'm completely committed to you!

"But I feel a strain, and it seems to come from the Anchor. Why do I feel that?"

Because you see the shore and you're anxious to get there. What you don't see are the rocks beneath the surf. What you

feel as restriction is actually security.

I let that statement rumble around in my heart. How many times would my life have been dashed upon the rocks if not for the security of that "more-than-able" Anchor? How many times would I have veered off course and lost my way except that I was able to drop that Anchor so I could pause and catch my bearings?

Another wave of truth hits my boat.

An anchor isn't just for use in the rough waters—it's to use for times of rest as well.

I have a wonderful memory of being on a catamaran off the coast of Kauai. The wind and waves were very high that day, so the captain found a sheltered bay and lowered the anchor. We were able to have lunch and snorkel straight off the boat away from the pounding surf. My life hasn't been one big storm. Many days and seasons have been calm and easy going. But, just like that day in Kauai, I still needed a place to rest! God, my Anchor, is there for me in my rest, too. That thought floods my heart with peace.

"Do I need to know about how you work as my Anchor?"

Much more, but it comes down to this: Your Anchor gives your life purpose and direction. You haven't been left to drift wherever the current pleases. You get to chart a course, and the Anchor helps you to stay on that course.

A sense of purpose and meaning for my life washes over me in a big wave. I feel hope soak through me. If I can lean on this understanding that God is my Anchor and that he is fully committed to me and my journey, then where can I go that he won't be there to guide me?

Knowing that God is my Anchor gives me security, purpose, direction, and a place to rest. Those are the desires and cries of my heart. When I'm feeling "off," it's because I don't feel secure in a situation or because of the waters in which I find myself. If I feel directionless, like there's no sign of land on the horizon, it may be that I've been in the waves too long without a place to rest. The reality that God, my Anchor, will secure me is overwhelming. It dares me to dream of how far I can travel on this earth. The sense of restriction is replaced by a feeling of freedom. I can actually chart a course and, with the help of my Anchor, get there.

God is my Anchor, and he isn't holding me back, he's calling me out. My heart needed to know that today.

Day 4

✠

who am i to you?

We'll want to ask much more about God's identity during this forty-day journey. But for now, pause to listen concerning your own identity before him. We get many conflicting and condemning messages about ourselves from the world, the flesh, and the devil. Our mind often hears "old tapes" and speaks negative self-talk.

But to walk in spiritual and emotional health, we need to defer to Jesus. To rephrase his question to the Apostle Peter, "who does he say that you are?" He wants to speak a living word to your heart that will undermine your tendency toward self-loathing or false humility. True humility is simply agreeing with God about who you are. So let's ask him, "Lord, how would you finish the following sentence concerning me: 'You are my _____.'?"

Now consider this: What if God's answer is true? How does that influence your self-worth? Your self-talk? Does knowing this change how you live or think? Find out by taking time today to be what and who Jesus says you are.

who am i to you?

I feel about as comfortable asking Jesus who I am to him as I have ever felt on a first date—butterflies and all! I want to figure this out for myself, but after yesterday, I realize it's not about figuring things out on my own, it's about asking God and then letting him answer. So where will we meet to discuss this?

Jesus and I are meeting at a coffee shop today. I walk in the door and see he's saving a couple of seats right by the fire. The chairs are cozy, and I ease into the one across from him. We exchange smiles.

"Have you been waiting long?" I ask.

Just a few minutes. I like getting here early and anticipating your arrival.

I think I actually feel myself blush at his sweet comment. With that, two hot drinks arrive, my favorite and his.

"You ordered for me?"

It's your favorite, isn't it?

"Yes."

Remember, I'm attentive. I noticed you like chai lattés.

We laugh easily together and then fall into a comfortable silence. I wonder how to pose the question, afraid it'll just sound silly. Someone walks by, recognizes Jesus, and comes over to say "Hi." Jesus talks with her and then turns toward me.

Let me introduce my friend Eden to you...

The word "friend" and all the strings attached to it race to the front of my thoughts. But before I start trying to figure things out, I decide to wait until she leaves and then let Jesus answer my questions.

"You called me your friend. Why?"

Because you are. Don't you think we are? I don't meet for a chai latté with someone who isn't my friend. Those meetings are usually held somewhere cold and impersonal. But you and I, we connect. You've opened your heart to me, and that's all I require of a friend.

Our eyes meet over our steaming drinks, and I realize that I believe him. I am his friend, and he is mine!

"When did that happen? I mean, when did we become friends?"

When you stopped trying to be good and started being real.

"That wasn't easy. I'm still not sure how real I am at times. It seems way easier to measure goodness than 'realness'."

That's probably true, because the world and the church have put up so many measuring sticks to determine 'goodness.' But being real is highly underrated. Being real looks messy sometimes, but that's the risk you take in being my friend. Is it worth it?

"Being real is the most amazing thing I have ever experienced. I always thought it would be like being naked in front of everyone, completely exposed. I was trying to cover myself with the 'garments of goodness,' but those garments never really warmed or protected me. Being real, being known, is the most liberating action I have ever taken."

I've robed you in the garment of friendship, Eden. Is it warm?

"Very!"

Do you feel protected?

"Like never before!"

I slide back into the comfort of my chair, put my feet up, and smile across the table at Jesus, my Friend.

Day 5

✠

how do you see me?

By now, you've heard God tell you who you are to him. Perhaps he called you his beloved son or daughter, his faithful servant or precious friend. Now let's borrow his spiritual eyes to ask, "How do you see me?"

One day when I asked God this question, I saw an oyster shell and concluded automatically that God sees the pearl of the kingdom that he's placed in my heart. But he said, "No, Brad, that's not it. While the pearl is precious, you believe too easily that I only love you because I see something perfect that I've planted within you—something that's not really you. But I'm showing you the oyster, because I'm fascinated by the shell. I see that unique, bumpy shell as your personality. I'm intrigued by the way life has shaped you. I like you. I think you're a keeper. I think I'll put you in my collection."

How does God see you? Ask him why. And be wary of jumping to conclusions like I did. Do you have the humility to agree with God? What if what he tells you is true? How does that affect how you see yourself?

how do you see me?

Jesus and I are standing at the edge of a beautiful garden. A wrought iron fence surrounds the garden, and a path extends from the gate into the unseen beauty within.

We stand at the gate for what seems like a very long time. Jesus doesn't seem to be in any hurry. Again, I feel awkward about asking a question that puts the spotlight on me, but I trust Jesus' answers are what I need to hear. I'm fearful, so I reach out to take his hand. He receives it with a squeeze.

Let's sit down for a few minutes, Eden.

There's a bench near the garden gate, so we sit down on it and enjoy the shade of a large tree. I fight back fear as I pose my question.

"Jesus, how do you see me?"

A smile crosses his lips, and he rubs his hands together in anticipation.

I thought you might never ask. I love this question!

And then he pauses.

Are you hungry?

"What?"

Are you hungry?

"A little, maybe. Why do you ask?"

I brought something along.

He steps behind the tree and emerges a moment later with a picnic basket. I can see that he's excited about what he's put together, and it makes me feel happy that he prepared for our meeting. He opens the lid of the picnic basket and pulls out a blanket for us to sit on. I get off the bench and join him on the blanket. Then he begins to pull out all sorts of dishes and containers, spreading them out on the blanket. By the time he's pulled everything out, there is barely room left for him and I to sit.

Then, just when I think Jesus might have forgotten my question, he turns to me.

No, you aren't a picnic!

A quick laugh escapes my mouth. He has put me right at ease.

But I do see you as a picnic basket.

"Tell me why."

You are a container, a vessel that can hold many things. You have been packing your own picnic for years, careful to make sure that you had everything you thought you needed. Do you see how much I pulled out of this basket? You can hold a lot!

"Is that good or bad?"

Both. It's bad when you pack it full of what *you* think you need. You and I have been spending the last few months unpacking your basket, taking out all the things you don't need. There were a lot of things in your basket that were just weighing you down. They had no good purpose in your life.

But if you let *me* pack the picnic basket, it's a good thing. I want to fill you up with all kinds of good things. Will you let me?

"Of course!"

I don't just want to fill your basket; I want you to enjoy the gifts that I put inside. Let me show you how to partake in them throughout the day.

Day 6

✠

Do you love me?
how much?

You've probably heard or read many times that Jesus loves you. But has he ever told you this himself? I believe he wants to tell you this today. In fact, I believe he longs to do this. God knows that hearing about his love as mere information will never satisfy the human heart. Only a heartfelt declaration from his own lips can do this.

Truth only becomes real once it is believed and experienced. This happens best when you look God in the face (with the eyes of your heart) and ask him, "Do you love me? How much do you love me? Why do you love me? What does your love for me look like?"

Our flesh tries to dismiss God's love as "just hearing what we want to hear," thus ending the conversation immediately. Don't be fooled. God does speak, especially about his feelings for you. So engage the Lord on this theme, remembering that God's love is immeasurably long, wide, high, and deep. There's always more, so never be afraid to seek out his affirmation. Experiencing God's love is crucial for our well being.

Do you love me?
how much?

I find myself needing to meet with Jesus in a warm location this morning. The house feels cold, and I'm chilled in spite of the blankets in which I'm wrapped. Maybe I can warm myself from the inside out by meeting with Jesus on a warm, sunny beach.

In a moment, I'm there with not another soul in sight. Turquoise waves lap at the white sand, and a warm, tropical breeze soothes my weariness. The intensity of the sun's rays warm my back, and I relax.

I look around for Jesus, curious where he might be in this paradise. I see him swinging in a hammock between two enormous palm trees. I make my way over to him, the sand warming my feet a little more than I needed.

He sits up as I approach and swings his legs over the side of the hammock, turning it into a swinging couch with room for two. I make myself comfortable beside him.

I'm glad you came. This is such a perfect place for you to hear what I have to say.

"But I thought I was the one asking the questions."

I don't want you to have to ask, I want you to learn how to hear me saying this all the time. I never stop saying and demonstrating it to you. Ready?

"I'm not sure."

Why?

"Because I want to believe you, but I know my heart will try to deny it."

When you learn to listen to me saying this all the time, your heart won't be able to deny it anymore.

"I don't want to deny it; I want to live in the truth."

Good, then you're ready! I love you!

The sincerity in his eyes causes tears to blur my vision.

Can you feel that truth going into your heart? I love you!

I can feel it, but I'm a bit overwhelmed by the intensity of his words.

I love you so much that I spend my time thinking up new ways to tell you over and over again.

A smile creeps across my face. "I think I noticed. You've really been pulling out all the stops lately."

Then why are you so uncomfortable and ready to deny my love for you?

His words test my heart, and I'm not sure I'm even able to answer. "I really don't want to. It's just my default mode when I'm given something I don't think I deserve."

Love is my gift to you. It's not about deserving it; it's about receiving it. I want to pour it out on you, and I want you to enjoy its warmth. Would you like to have some more?

"As much as you can spare!"

There's no end to it, Eden. *I am* love. I won't run out of it or shortchange anyone else if I give it to you. I want to pour out my love extravagantly on you. Look at the waves lapping upon the shore. My love is even more consistent than their constant rhythm. Let my love wash over you like waves.

Just then the spray from a big wave hits me. I smile as I taste the salty water running down my face, knowing it's no longer my tears.

Day 7

✠

Do you like me?
why Do you like me?

I believe God loves me. After all, God is Love. That's his very nature. He loves the most unlovable people on the earth.

But to believe he really likes me? That's another matter. I often feel very unlikable, which leads me to feel sorry for God. He says he is with us all the time and that he will never leave us or forsake us. Yikes. When I'm not doing very well, I wonder how he can stand to be near me much less enjoy my company.

As I was mulling over this problem one day, my friend Rob sidled up to me and said, "Brad, I have a message for you from God. He says, 'I like you.'" That stunned me. "How can you say that?" I wondered to God. But there was no shaking it. I felt a deep assurance in my heart that God is quite happy to be stuck with me.

As you listen to God today, ask him the following questions: "Do you like me? Why do you like me? What do you see that's likeable?" I guarantee you will be surprised at his response!

Do you like me?
Why do you like me?

As much as I need to be loved, I also need to be liked. When someone tells me they like me, I take it as both a compliment and a blessing. I like to be liked!

I know that Christians are supposed to love one another, but sometimes we don't even like each other. Sometimes, I wonder if God feels the same way about us!

I can still see the waves that are a vivid reminder of the consistency of his love for me. But does he like me? And if so, what does he like about me?

I need to find him. "Where are you, Jesus?"

The eyes of my heart focus, and I can see where Jesus is standing. Of course, he never really left, I just needed to look for him in the midst of my busyness. There he is across a very busy aisle in a store. Our eyes meet through all of the people between us, and our recognition of each other is evidenced by our smiles. I begin to work my way toward him, dropping all the things I have collected at my feet and opening my arms to embrace him. Our embrace lasts a bit longer than is probably appropriate for "in-store" hugs, but I'm just so glad to see him in the midst of all this chaos.

"Jesus. What are you doing here?" I ask.

I was hoping to find you here! Are you almost done?

"I've got an idea," I reply. "Follow me." We make our way through several departments of the store until we find ourselves in the furniture section. I find what looks like the coziest couch of the lot and invite Jesus to join me on it.

"So why were you looking for me?"

Because I like you, and I just thought it would be nice to be around you!

"Really? I'm just beginning to realize how much I like you, too" We sit there looking at each other with ridiculous grins on our faces. "What do you like about me?"

I like that you can find me in a busy store. I like that you drop things to be with me. I like that you ask me questions and wait to hear my answer. I like that you choose the coziest couch in the whole store. Do you need to hear more?

"I'd love to, but can I tell you why I like you?"

Okay!

"I like that you show yourself to me in a busy store. I like that you surprise me with unexpected treats and gifts. I like that you put thought into our times together, that you plan ahead for me. I like you, because I feel happier and lighter and more grounded after we've had time together. Do you need to hear more?"

I'd love to, but can I tell you more first?

"Go ahead."

I like you, because you include me. I like the way you smile at me and the way your eyes light up when you see me or sense

my presence. It makes my heart glad. I like being liked, too!

As we talk, I realize this little impromptu meeting may take longer than expected. I may even have to buy the couch!

Day 8

✠

show me my heart

What does your heart look like? The great saints described the heart as God's dwelling place—his temple or throne room. Some were more expansive than that, seeing the heart as a glorious city or a great kingdom. In John 14, when Jesus says that his Father's house has many mansions, some believe the Father's house he was referring to is the Church, in which every Christian heart represents one of the mansions in which Jesus dwells.

Others see their hearts as disheveled homes that are badly in need of Christ's renovation skills. They invite his healing light to illuminate dark corners and cleanse secret closets of old junk.

Today, ask God to show you a picture of your heart. Invite him to give you a tour. What do you see? What does it mean? Don't try to figure it out—ask him. Then ask him to transform your heart into a place of refuge. He is willing to repair what was broken and restore what was lost. He has chosen to make your heart his eternal home, so you might as well give him the run of the place now.

show me my heart

There have been extended times in my life when I would not have been able to ask this question. Fear of what the answer might be would have prevented me from pursuing God for a response. But as we've deepened our friendship, God has shown me that there was never any need for fear. I was afraid he might use some cruel or revealing symbol to describe my heart, like an empty balloon or a piece of rotten fruit, but I know now he would never do that.

God has been revealing my heart to me over the past three months, and while it isn't pretty, it is full of hope. My heart is like a yard. When he first walked through it with me, it looked all right. The grass was short, it was roomy, and it was very simple in its layout. But that same night, he pulled up in a backhoe and began to dig up my heart's yard. Of course, the practical side of me didn't want a mess. "Leave what's buried, buried," were my sentiments. But God had other plans, and I had to make a choice.

It all came down to this: God was going to unearth things in my heart. I could either lie down in protest and be crushed by the backhoe or climb up into the cab and join him on this adventure. I chose to join him, and three months into the journey, I can say I have no regrets!

Right now, my heart is pock-marked with a seemingly random series of holes of varying depths, beside which are piles of dirt. I suspect the holes aren't random at all, and that someday I will view them from a different vantage point that will allow me to see more clearly what God has been creating. For now, I let him lead me through the yard, taking it on faith that everything we're looking at has a purpose.

Some of the holes Jesus has dug hold memories to which I needed to return for healing. Some holes are quite shallow, really. Others go rather deep. Still other holes hold treasures that I had buried years earlier—desires, preferences, and gifts. I had set them aside, and, eventually, they had become buried and overgrown.

Some of those expeditions into my heart have been painful, like when the dentist's drill goes a bit too far before the freezing kicks in. Others have felt like Christmas. Overall, the dramatic change my heart has experienced through letting God explore it is astonishing. By providing me with a way to describe my heart, an image of what it looks like, God has helped me feel free enough to let him dig for what I didn't know was buried.

My heart is a yard. It *was* simple and neat. It is *now* messy and in transition. But I trust God, my Excavator, to finish what he has started, to redeem what was lost, to decontaminate the soil, to unearth hidden treasures, and, ultimately, to restore Eden.

Day 9

✠

Do you have a gift for me today?

As if we haven't already gorged ourselves on God's blessings, dare we also ask him for yet another gift? Yes! In fact, we dare not think ourselves above the need for daily grace. Remember that God is a Blesser by nature. It brings him joy to give good and perfect gifts to his children.

More importantly, when we neglect to come before God with open, expectant hands, we have a nasty habit of looking elsewhere for our needs to be met. When David sinned with Bathsheba, God's rebuke is telling: "I gave you Saul's house, Saul's wives, and Saul's kingdom. If that were not enough, I would have given you more!" (2 Samuel 12:8). David fell, because he stopped asking God and started taking from other sources.

Today, come before the Lord with open hands. See what he puts inside of them. What gift is he giving you? If it is some type of symbolic object, ask him what it means. Ask him what it's for. And, if necessary, don't forget to ask for batteries and instructions!

Do you have a gift for me today?

In the past few weeks, I have received more gifts than any one person should be allowed. I have been showered with praise and affection, lavished with love, and filled up with encouragement. And yet now I find myself asking for even more. Is this okay?

"Jesus where do you want to meet today?"

He is in our living room, a cozy and familiar setting for me. I sit down on the couch beside him and take a moment to appreciate his presence.

"I'm so glad you're willing to be here. I love when your presence is in our house."

I love being invited!

"I have some questions for you. Do you mind?"

Go ahead.

"I'm supposed to ask you for a gift, but I feel kind of greedy doing so. You know how much I've received in the past few weeks. Is there a point where I just have to say, 'enough'?"

Yes, but let me be the one that says 'enough,' not you.

"Okay. But why?"

Because I'm far more generous than you or anyone else. You say 'enough' far too quickly.

"Then if I'm not being greedy, and you have good gifts for me, what gift do you have for me today?"

I want you to have a blanket of peace. I've noticed your peace level is a little low, and I want you to walk through this season in peace.

"Tell me what peace looks like. I'm not so sure I really know anymore."

Peace looks like this: You're in the middle of a chaotic setting, maybe it's getting the boys off to school or shopping, or maybe it's just being bombarded with demands on your time. It doesn't matter which chaotic scenario you choose or even if it is all that chaotic. Peace in the middle of those things looks like me walking on the water. It's knowing that I'm right there with you. There is nothing that can separate you from me. *That* knowledge will bring the peace you need.

"So that means when the world is crashing in on me and I start to feel overwhelmed, I can climb under my peace blanket and hide?"

Not exactly. Sometimes it might mean that you curl up for a while under the blanket, giving yourself time and space to feel my presence. But you can wear your blanket of peace anytime, anywhere. That means you can pull it around you and be covered in the middle of those chaotic situations, and they will no longer be chaotic in your heart.

"So peace is being aware of your presence?"

My presence ushers in peace.

"Thanks for this good gift. I can see where I need it—a lot! You're very generous, and if you have more good gifts to give me, then I want them all. I don't want to be the one saying 'enough,' I want to be the one who asks for more."

That makes me happy! You've been unwilling to receive my gifts for a long time. But I have other things I've been longing to give. I can't wait to see you open some of these gifts I've been saving up for you, and I can't wait to see you use them. Gifts are a good thing, Eden!

As I pull the blanket of peace closer, I feel his arms surround me.

day 10

✠

what gift can i offer you today?

For those feeling a little guilty lately about receiving such abundant affection from the Lord, today's question may come as a bit of a relief. We will ask him if there is a gift that he would like from us. Not that he needs anything—talk about shopping for the One who has everything! And I'm sorry, but you probably won't surprise him, either. Nevertheless, he will take you up on your offer.

So let's ask: "Lord, what gift can I bring to so great a King? Is there some symbolic object I might lay at your feet or some favor you would appreciate from me? How can I say thanks for the blessings you've poured out on me (Psalm 116:12)? Is there some way I can bless you in return?"

Then watch and listen to how the Lord responds. Feel free to discuss his request with him. In particular, you might want to ask why that particular gift will bless him today.

what gift can i offer you today?

No one knows the poverty of my heart more than God. I struggle to find something that would be worthy to be called a gift. I don't believe this is false humility. I'm just having a difficult time believing there is anything I could give to my Redeemer that wouldn't be lacking.

I'm standing before the throne, staring up into the eyes of my King. My surroundings and my King fill me with awe. His throne is enormous, beautiful, and inviting. My King extends his hand to me, not like some royalty condescending to a commoner but like a father opening up his arms to his child. I feel no intimidation as I respond to his invitation.

Welcome, Eden.

I smile in response.

Where would you like to sit?

"As close to you as possible."

Then crawl up here on my lap.

I feel no shame in being a grown woman sitting on God's lap. It seems as natural as if I were a little girl. I feel so secure.

"I want to offer you a gift, but I feel like I've come empty-handed."

Let's see what you've got.

I squirm—really feeling like a little girl now—unsure where to begin. Do I pull out all of my little childish toys and let him root through them or do I lay out my rock collection for him to be dazzled by? My options feel limited and sadly lacking.

Eden, quit looking for the gift in your pockets. What I want is in your heart.

"I thought that was where I was looking. I just can't find anything that seems special enough to give to you. Everything just looks old, tired or broken, I want your gift to be new and shiny."

Let *me* take a look.

I look down, and it's as if he has turned my heart into a treasure chest. I can see the clasp that keeps it closed, and I'm afraid he may find it's empty when he opens it. But my King doesn't show that same fear.

Will you open it for me, Eden?

I fumble with the latch, even though it swings open easily, then raise the lid. I'm amazed to see there are all kinds of treasures within. Not everything looks valuable. Some of the items do look like broken toys and rock collections, but it is full. I turn to Jesus in surprise.

"How did these get in here?"

I've been depositing things in your heart for years.

"*You* put all of this in here?"

Not all of it, just the good stuff.

I push the treasure chest toward him. "You can have anything you want, but if you choose something you put in, isn't that like buying your own gift?"

Have you ever bought a gift for someone and really liked it yourself?"

I nod.

Everything I deposit into your heart, I like. That's why I put it there. I'm trying to make your heart a collection of my favorite things.

"Well then, what do you want? You can take anything you like."

I want it all!

"All the good stuff?"

I want it all!

I shove the treasure chest, my heart, into his hands.

"Then I really want you to have it!"

Day 11

✠

what gift can i offer others today?

After receiving gifts from God and responding with gifts to him, let's pause to look outward. Spirituality that remains solely internal fulfills only the first of the two greatest commandments. We want to love God with heart, mind, and strength, but we also want to love our neighbor in God's name. In fact, both James and John suggest in their epistles that one cannot truly obey either of these commandments without also obeying the other (1 John 3:17; James 2:14ff). As I've suggested elsewhere, there is a spiritual respiration in healthy Christians, by which we inhale the love of God into our hearts and then exhale it into the lives of others.

So let's ask God, "What gift can I offer others today? How and with whom shall I share it?" With this step, listening prayer becomes practical, but it also takes us deeper into the heart of God. We can only begin to know what makes God tick when we begin to share his selfless love with others.

what gift can i
offer others today?

My mind races as I try to figure out who will be the recipient of my gift. And what will the gift be? A sea of faces stretches out in front of me, threatening to drown out God's voice in my heart.

"Jesus, I need you to come into my busy heart and mind."

Here he comes, walking on the waves that roll across that sea. Calmly, he rises above all those possibilities, and my frantic figuring ceases. He comes alongside me, and we sit together on a large rock overlooking the sea.

"I want to give someone a gift today, to bless them somehow. But I'd like you to choose who that person is. Will you please choose someone from this sea of faces? I can't seem to do it myself."

I'd love to help you, Eden. But first, I want you to know that the biggest part of this exercise has already been accomplished. The crucial factor in the giving of a gift is the willingness of the giver to give it. It takes effort on your part to overcome your own wants and focus on what someone else might need. These gifts that you give, gift that I periodically ask you to deliver, are not extravagances. Yes, the person may have been able to get through the day or the week or even their entire life without your gift. But what I ask you to give is still very necessary! Have you ever received a gift that made your day? That's because it was exactly what you needed at that moment, even if you didn't realize it at the

time. Let's do that for someone else today.

"Just one? Look at all those faces out there."

You're not the only giver, Eden. I don't have to depend solely on you.

"Right. Show me who you want me to give a gift to today, and what it is you want me to give."

Jesus walks purposefully to the edge of the sea and picks up one of the many faces there. He brings it back and sits down with me again. I look at the chosen face.

"I don't recognize that face, Jesus. How can I give a gift to someone I don't recognize?"

In this way: Many people in this world are no longer recognized. They walk in and around this world and are never noticed by anyone else. Their hearts long to be noticed, to be seen, to be appreciated. Today, one of those people will walk across your path. The gift I want you to give them is recognition.

"How do I deliver that?"

By engaging them with eye contact. Look into them, Eden. Let your eyes tell them, 'I see you! I notice you! Jesus recognizes you!'

"I can do that."

You'll have to be watchful. It's easy for them to cross your path without being noticed. They've made a habit of it.

"Would you help me find them? Will you walk my path with me today?"

I'd love to.

He takes my hand, and we follow the path together.

Day 12

✠

whats on your heart, God?

Whenever I sing choruses that proclaim "It's all about you, Jesus," I admit to feeling a measure of guilty cynicism. Why? Because when t comes to my prayer life, the truth is, it's usually all about me. I talk with God about my needs, *my* sins, *my* burdens, *my* family, *my* church, *my* ministry, and so on.

But have you ever considered that God might like to share what's on his heart? Would you like to know what excites him and brings him pleasure? Would you like to know what grieves or troubles his Spirit? Does that matter to you? Can he confide in you as an intimate friend?

A while back, the Lord told me that it grieves him whenever he tries to share his burdens with me and I slide immediately into a guilt trip. He told me it is just further evidence that our relationship is still all about me. Ouch! But it spurred me to ask, "Okay, Lord, please take your turn. What's on your heart today? Is there anything joyful or sad you'd share with me? And why does this thing make you rejoice or mourn? I really want to hear." Why don't you try asking God these same questions today?

whats on your heart, God?

I feel shame creep over me as I realize how little I ask God this question. But I will not allow shame to rob me of asking him today or rob God of having an audience with a willing listener. I'll shake off the cloak that threatens to make *my* heart more important than my Maker's, find him, ask him, and then listen to what he says.

"Where are you, God?"

Immediately, I can see one of the very first meeting places I ever had with God. It's a simple hut with a dirt floor and nothing inside but two stools on which to sit. The hut has two open doors that face each other, allowing bright sunshine to stream inside. As I approach, I can see God's silhouette on one of the stools as he waits for me. He turns to watch me as I near this humble dwelling. I step inside the doorway and feel immediately a sense of "being home." I embrace my Maker, and if there is any remnant of shame left on my back, it falls to the ground during that embrace and lies powerless at our feet.

We sit down on the stools and face one another with very little distance between us. The moment feels so intimate that I barely want to speak, but I want to hear his answer.

"Father, what's on your heart today?" I finally manage to ask.

My Son's birthday.

"Your Son's birthday?"

Yes, you know it's coming up.

"Hmm. But why would it be on your heart? Aren't there world issues and serious ethical problems that would take up more of your heart's space?"

Not today. My heart is occupied with my Son's birthday.

This revelation makes me grin. I feel like laughing, not because I think it's silly, but because my Maker cares about his Son's birthday! I have just gained a whole new insight into who God the Father is.

"What about his birthday occupies your heart?

His birthday always floods me with memories. You may never have thought of this, but I have experienced the pain of childbirth. It was not an easy thing to bring Jesus into this world. Imagine all the things I wanted to give him but couldn't, all the ways I wanted to protect him but couldn't. He was so small and vulnerable. My Son was fully man, a human, a baby, and I had to give him up at birth. Of course, I tried to choose good parents, but they were untested. And there were so many tests along the journey for all three of them... So many prophecies to fulfill. Jesus' birthday was a glorious day! My heart loves to go there.

"So does mine, even more so now! What did you enjoy most about his birthday?"

Besides the moment that he actually entered this world, I think my favorite moment was the choir of angels that proclaimed his birth. It was the only extravagance I gave him that night, and, in spite of his humble birthplace, he was born a king! The choir of angels reflected that.

"I'm so glad I asked you this question. Your answer has made my Christmas. Thank you!"

Day 13

✠

What in me causes you grief?

For the next six days, we'll ask God more specifically what is on his heart. We'll cover both his joys and sorrows concerning ourselves, our families, our churches, and our nations.

You should also feel free to ask God about other emotions he feels, such as what angers him or what he's looking forward to. Actually, I love asking God what he's nervous about. He always says, "Nothing!" And I find that gives me a lot of peace.

I'd also encourage you to ask God how he feels about other groups with which you identify, such as your fellow employees, community members or even humankind as a whole.

But let's start closer to home. "Lord, is there anything in my life that causes you sorrow? Please show me. What needs to happen in that area so you no longer feel that way about it? What response are you looking for from me in that area?"

what in me
causes you grief?

That I have caused God grief there is no question. How many times? Countless I'm sure. But I want to be specific about the state of my heart today.

"I need you here, Father. Can you show yourself to me?"

Immediately, I see him in my heart's yard sitting on the swing. He waves for me to come close. I feel reluctance as I approach, like a child who knows she is going to get a spanking. Somehow I continue to move forward and, eventually, I'm standing before him. Maybe this is, in small measure, what Judgment Day will feel like. Unable to look into my Father's wonderful eyes, I focus on his feet and shift my weight from one foot to the other.

"I have a question for you, Father," I finally stammer. "What in me causes you grief?"

Please look at me, Eden.

I fight back the fear that claws at me, but I know what I'll see in those eyes. And so courage grows within, and, finally, I raise my eyes to gaze into his. Tears stand ready to testify to my anxiousness over his answer to this question.

Let's sit down.

He takes my hand and leads me to sit down beside him.

Do you remember what you called this swing when it first

appeared in your heart's yard?

"Yes. My redemption swing."

Good, then this is the perfect place to ask me this question. So what are you more afraid of: me or my answer?

"You."

***That* grieves me, Eden.**

My tears are no longer hidden from sight. They have begun a slow descent down my face, and I'm unable to control them. My throat closes up, and I know that even if I could talk, my voice would be thin and high-pitched. I manage a whispered, "I'm sorry!"

Do you want to know *why* it grieves me?

I nod.

It grieves me, because I feel closer to you than ever. I feel like you know me better than ever. We have faced so many things together, worked on so many issues in your life, and discovered so many new gifts and promises in your heart. We have walked together every day in this last year; and yet somehow you still have fear that I will be harsh or heavy-handed or act without mercy. I'm grieved, because you still haven't fully experienced my heart for you.

My tears are accompanied by shudders, but I also feel relief now, not fear. He has demonstrated his heart for me in this very moment. There is nothing cruel or unjust about how he has shared his answer.

"Can you redeem my fear?" I finally ask, my voice quavering.

Always! Look where we're sitting.

Immediately, fear disappears from my heart like fog in the heat of the day. Instead of the spanking I was expecting, my Father allowed me to see yet another piece of his heart instead. Amazing grace! Amazing mercy! Amazing love!

Day 14

✠

what in me
brings you joy?

You are probably much harder on yourself than God is. Am I right? Many who read this know that some measure of self-hatred is still operating in their life. We tend to reserve our harshest judgments for ourselves in the mistaken belief that this will protect us from pride. But, as TV's Dr. Phil would say, "How's that working out for you?"

The good news is, when God thinks about you, he's generally smiling. He knows you well enough to look past your faults and see the treasure that is you. You bring him great joy. And it's not just some vague sense that you're okay. He sees specific aspects of your life journey that thrill him so much he often bursts into song. Don't believe it? Go ahead and ask him! "What are you seeing in me today that brings you joy? Where in my life am I getting it right? What fruits of the Spirit are starting to sprout? What in my life would cause you to clap for me or pat me on the back?"

what in me
brings you joy?

Why does it always seem like the glass is half-empty when it comes to finding the good stuff inside of me? I am very aware of my sin and shortcomings, but my gifts and talents hide from my sight and leave me questioning whether I have any at all. I know I have caused God grief, and large amounts of it at that. But that I have caused him joy seems a stretch. Why does this battle carry on in my heart? Is there something I'm missing?

"Jesus?"

Once again, I see Jesus sitting in the redemption swing in the shade. He looks pleased with himself, like he has something he wants to tell me and has been keeping it to himself for a while. I walk toward him through my heart's yard, never removing my gaze from his. Just before I reach him, Jesus rises from the swing and opens his arms with a great sweeping motion. I fall into them, and they close around me tightly. I don't make any attempt to break the embrace. I could stay here forever.

I have no idea how long we stand there clinging to each other, but, eventually, Jesus draws me to the swing and we sit close together.

"What in me causes you joy?" I ask, fighting back the urge to qualify the question with statements that won't put Jesus on the hook. The glass is still half-empty.

My joy is entwined in your joy. Let me ask you a question in

return. What gives you joy?

"I get joy out of being with my boys, laughing with them over jokes, comforting them with cuddles, and sharing life with them in general. I also get joy out of knowing that I heard you right, that I obeyed you, and that everything went as it should have gone, if only for a few minutes. I get joy out of looking into people's eyes and seeing you there. Joy bubbles up and threatens to overflow my heart's banks when I watch our wonderful friends worship with freedom on Monday mornings."

> **That wasn't hard was it? Why do you think I wouldn't find you to be a source of joy as well?**

I have no answer.

> **When I see you with your boys, hugging, cuddling, joking, playing, comforting, and sharing life, that gives me joy. When you recognize my voice and obey and all goes as planned, if only for a few minutes, that gives me joy. When you see me in the eyes of others and there's that moment of recognition, that brings me joy. When I see how full your cup is as you watch our friends worship on Monday mornings, my heart nearly bursts with joy.**

> **Do you see how entwined my joy is with yours? Does that help you to see that the cup really is full?**

My heart is filled with wonder and joy at his response. My Father enjoys the same things I do! When my cup feels half-empty, I can just look to my own heart to see what brings me joy, and I'll know that my Father's joy is mixed in there as well.

I'm inspired to find all the things in my life that bring me joy just so that I can see the joy in my Father's eyes as well.

Day 15

✠

what in my family causes you grief?

Family relationships are a good, albeit harsh, test case of one's spirituality. You've probably heard such ominous proverbs as "If Christianity doesn't work at home, it doesn't work at all," or "If you want to know if your heart is at peace, ask your children." I know: "Oh brother!"

The Apostle John liked to use the following test: "If anyone says, 'I love God,' yet hates his brother, he is a liar. For anyone who does not love his brother, whom he has seen, cannot love God, whom he has not seen" (1 John 4:20). The fact is, you cannot use spirituality to hide from poor family relationships. We absolutely must talk to God about how to live as families.

Today, ask God, "What grieves you in my family? What can we do about this together?" It's a risky question, but it is also one that paves the way toward healing in your heart and in your family as a whole.

what in my family causes you grief?

"Father, I remember looking into the future as a young girl to see what my family would be like. Who would I marry? How many children would I have? Would I have boys or girls? Where would we live? What would we look like? Would we be happy?

"Now that I have lived out the answers to those questions, I can say without reserve that you have blessed me beyond my wildest hopes. To be honored with a godly husband and gifted with three amazing boys is my dream come true. I would not trade lives with *anyone*. This is what I was made for!

"But within this dream lies the reality that we are not perfected yet, that we still struggle within these bodies to do what is good and right. If there are dynamics within the relationships of my family that cause you grief, then I want to hear about them, to face them, and to ask for your help to correct them.

"Father? Where will we meet?"

I see him standing on the foundation of a house. I can't quite tell whether it's an old foundation or a new foundation, but there he is, standing in the middle of it calling me to join him. I approach him with joy in my heart and open my arms to embrace him just as he opens his arms to me.

"I love you. You're a good Father."

I love you. And I love *being* your Father.

"Father, you know I love my life and you know I love my family, but I have to ask a difficult question: Is there anything that causes you grief in our family? Please answer gently; these are the jewels in my crown."

They're jewels in my crown, too, carefully chosen jewels. That would be where my grief lies. You are a family of jewels, each one precious, each one unique, and each one necessary to complete the set. But sometimes you lose sight of each other's value. When that happens, you lose sight of me, and that makes me grieve.

"What can we do to change that?"

Shine each other up. Draw out the preciousness of one another rather than pointing out the flaws. Within each one of you are wonderful surprises, gifts I've hidden from the world but are there to be discovered by those who really care. Be purposeful in searching for those gifts I've hidden. Enjoy the moment you find them, celebrate the gift, the giver, and the vessel that has carried each precious treasure. Build up rather than tear down.

My focus changes to the foundation on which we are standing.

"Is this a new foundation or an old one?" I ask.

It's ancient. It's the foundation on which I want your family to build. It's the foundation on which I built my family, a foundation of love and respect and 'being for each other.' Would you like to build on this foundation?

"Yes. When can we start?"

How about today?

Day 16

✠

What in my family brings you joy?

God is fully aware of the dysfunctions in your family, but he is just as tuned in to the treasures. He sees the little things you do right and the grand plans he has in store for you and yours. While we tend to focus on our failures, God is always able to ponder our families with great joy.

When we ask God what causes him joy in our families—our spouse, our parents, our children, our siblings—an awesome little miracle is activated. God deposits a very special kind of love in our hearts, and we begin to cherish one another even more. Simply by seeing God's joy in our families, we are stirred with fresh love for one another. We actually become more patient, more gentle, and more kind in our treatment of family members. Imagine! And this all starts not by trying harder (So frustrating!) but by listening to how your family brings God joy. Why not give it a try today?

what in my family brings you joy?

Father, I thank you for my family. I love spending time together as a group, and I love spending time with each member individually. They each contribute something rich to my life. They're a source of joy to me, and I hope they are a source of joy to you as well.

Today, feels a bit like the time I first introduced Brad to my parents. I was head over heels in love with him, and I wanted my parents to love him, too. I was looking for their approval of my choice, of the one I had chosen to love.

When we had children, I wanted my parents to love them like I did. It fed my heart when I watched them fuss and cuddle and love each of our babies. And my joy level rises when I see they still love our children now that they're older. It's that parental blessing for which we all long, which we all need. I think that's what I'm seeking from you today. I want to know there is something about our family that brings you joy, Father. Today, I will bring them all with me.

I can see Jesus waiting for us on the trampoline in our backyard. We all run toward it like it's a big race to see who can get there first. But, unlike a normal race, the sound that accompanies this pursuit is laughter. We all arrive at the same time and jump onto the trampoline to join Jesus, tumbling over each other until we finally settle into a comfortable tangle of arms and legs, Jesus right in the middle. We all sigh with the simple pleasure of being together.

"Father, is there anything in our family that brings you joy?" I ask once everyone has settled down.

This, right now, like this, brings me joy. That each of you can hear me and see me and spend time with me gives me great joy. That you include me in your days, that you are all aware of my presence, brings me joy. That I am a member of your family—with a voice—and that I am included in your daily lives brings me joy. That I'm also included in your decision-making is another source of great joy for me.

I'm pleasantly surprised by what joy our ragtag family can bring to Jesus. But why should I be surprised? He is the Father of each of us. And what good father doesn't feel joy at seeing his children so content?

"Thanks for being such a willing participant in our lives and in our family. We love having you as a part of us. You are so gracious to join us on our adventure in this world."

I love being a part of it!

Day 17

✠

What in my church causes you grief?

Just as we are often harder on ourselves than God is, we are also harder on our churches than our Father would like. He tends to be far more gracious than we are, and he has yet to give up on his Bride, as many of us are so quick to do. He's washing out spots, ironing out wrinkles, and preparing her gown for the big wedding day of his return. He isn't cynical about her, and he hasn't abandoned her. When he finally perfects and embraces her, will you be part of that divine hug?

When we ask God how our church might be grieving him, we must beware of picking up stones of accusation. Rather, we should identify with the sins of the people and then invite cleansing and healing. We are all members of the same body. Therefore, the sins of the church are really our sins. It doesn't take a prophet to know that we, the church, have really soiled ourselves. But God isn't looking to condemn us. He's looking for ears to hear what he wants to restore. Thus, we ask about his grief not so we can accumulate ammo but so we can repent and take up our calling in the world once again.

what in my church causes you grief?

This question has taken me three days to ask. I am very aware that I'm asking this question about the Bride of Christ. I don't want to listen with a critical ear. And I love my church! I love who we are, what we do, and where we're going. I feel like I need to hear this answer from the Bridegroom, the one who loves the Bride even more than I do. But still, it isn't easy to ask.

"Jesus, where will me meet today?"

I see him dressed for a wedding and standing at the front of our church. Our church meets in a school theatre, not a traditional church building, and that is where Jesus, the Bridegroom, now stands. As I approach him, I can sense the same pride I felt on my wedding day—the pride that I had chosen well! I can also see that Jesus is proud of his choice, his Bride, and that fills my heart with confidence to ask this hard question.

We sit down together at the front of the church. I realize I have not really looked at Jesus as the Bridegroom before, not to this extent, and he is breathtaking. Typical of a bride, I'm overwhelmed with my Bridegroom. He is altogether worthy of praise! What bride could ever measure up to this Bridegroom?

"Jesus, you amaze me! I could sit and gaze at you all day."

I'd like that. Your attention is just as full of worship to me as your words, songs, and actions.

My emotions start to spin within me. I feel like crying and then laughing. I feel peace and joy. I feel all kinds of emotions; not because I'm on some roller coaster, but because worship of him is drawing them out of me.

"Is there any stain on this bride's dress?" I finally ask.

Nothing I haven't already taken care of.

"But is there something that grieves you about her?"

Yes, there is. This Bride of mine is unaware of her beauty. She hides herself, because she thinks she's too dark. I am taken by her. I love her and am proud of who she is, how she looks, what she does. But she's reluctant to step out and be seen. I want to have her on my arm and parade her on the streets. I don't want to have to coax her out of this room.

"But we aren't like the other brides. We have people in our church that openly wear their pain and heartache. They might not even look like they're aware that they are part of a wedding celebration each week. I'm not sure that using the word 'beauty' to describe us is really the right word."

Then you haven't really seen the Bride yet. She is beautiful and confident of her position with the groom. My grief lies in her not being able to see that herself.

"Then I want to see her through *your* eyes Jesus."

Day 18

✠

what in my church brings you joy?

It's always good to practice seeing things through Jesus' eyes. This is especially important when it comes to the Church, because it helps us to see beyond surface issues to what God is really doing. Many church activities are nothing more than good human ideas that keep us busy. But whether God regrets it or not, he has thrown in his lot with us, so you can be sure he's also at work somewhere in the midst of your church and in the Bride of Christ as a whole. Can you see him? Ask him to show you what he's up to. The following questions will prove helpful:

"Lord, what in my church brings you joy? Why does it bring you joy? What activities in our church are you blessing right now? Are there ministries for which I should be praying? To which I should be giving? For which I should be serving?"

If you sense a particular area that is bringing joy to God's heart, please tell those involved. And don't forget to tell them why! Your words will likely strengthen God's servants just when they need it most.

what in my church brings you joy?

I love joy! It's so much deeper than just having a good day. It wells up like a spring directly from my heart and seeps into every part of my life. I want our church to bring joy to Jesus.

I can see Jesus, as the Bridegroom, sitting at the front doors to our church. He's in a wheelchair, but I'm not concerned about this at all. I know he isn't hurt or disabled in any way. I stand beside him and rest my hand on his shoulder. He reaches up to touch my hand and tugs me down beside him.

"Why are you in a wheelchair today, Jesus?" I ask.

Because it brings me joy.

My eyebrows bunch together in confusion. "Most people would see a wheelchair as a symbol of despair or hopelessness. Why does it bring you joy?"

It brings me joy, because so many wheelchairs occupy this church on Sunday mornings. But it isn't the wheelchairs that bring me the joy; it's the precious saints who fill them. Your little church, my Bride, has found a place for these saints to worship and declare their love for me. If you could only hear their hearts sing on Sunday mornings you would know how and why they bring me joy.

"Sometimes I think I hear whispers of it. Sometimes I get glimpses of the glory that surrounds them in their worship of you. I see how you have gifted them, that their hearts are in no way disabled, and how they minister to me and others. They bring me joy, too. What can we do to bring you more joy?"

Treasure these saints. Find places for them to belong. Accept them. Love them. Enjoy them. Defend them. Honor them. Hug them. Celebrate them. Celebrate with them. Be their friend. It's simple, really. They are your neighbors, and, even more than that, they are your brothers and sisters. Love your neighbor as yourself. Love your brother, love your sister.

"That doesn't seem very hard to do."

Yes, but there was a time when that was difficult for you, remember?

"Yes, I do. When we first planted Fresh Wind and these wonderful people started to join us week after week, I remember feeling some fear. I wasn't sure how to react to their gestures and vocalizing. There were so many uncertainties surrounding them. I really didn't know what to do."

You weren't the only one, Eden. Many people felt the same way. But that also brought me joy as I watched you all overcome your fears and embrace my saints. You didn't send them away or ask them to sit still and be quiet. You have recognized their hearts as whole, complete, and fully gifted, and that fills my heart with joy! It fills their hearts with joy, too.

Joy in my heart bubbles up and over. I feel like a well-watered garden whose springs won't fail (Isaiah 58:11).

83

Day 19

✠

what in my community or nation causes you grief?

Most Christians are better at complaining about their community, their government or the state of their nation than they are about praying for it. There is little doubt that the community and nation to which you belong and the governments that run them are grieving God in some way. But we don't get to sit back as armchair quarterbacks and critique others without somehow sharing in the responsibility. Even holy men like Daniel and Isaiah lamented with and for their people. "We have sinned," they said (Jeremiah 14:7; Daniel 9:5). They saw and confessed the sins of their nation as if they, themselves, had committed them. But the good news is, having repented as citizens of a sinful nation, God released mercy and grace.

Today, let's ask God, "What in my community or nation causes you grief? Why does it grieve you? How do you want me to respond? Shall I pray? Shall I speak out? Shall I act?" Then don't hestitate to do what he says.

what in my community or nation causes you grief?

I'm unwilling to take a single step into this arena without God right beside me.

"Father, where will we meet?"

I see a large map of our country, large enough to walk on, and right in the middle of it stands the Father. I walk until I'm standing right beside him.

"You have given all power and authority to the rulers of this world, and I know I have taken my share of shots at many of them. But today, I need to hear from you. I really don't want to listen with my own critical ear or political leanings. I want to know what grieves your heart about our nation."

What grieves me about this country is that it is full of selfish people. That isn't a new condition, and it may not even be that it's gotten worse. There are just more people to make the point. This nation is full of people who will go to any length to ensure their own rights are not violated but will trample over the rights of others in that pursuit. This is a nation full of people who know their own needs, demand to be helped, and expect that help to come quickly, even if it costs someone else. What grieves me most about this situation is that it never needed to happen. If this country would just take its eyes off itself, look around at what others need, and then step forward to help, it would be a much better place to live.

"It's true, I can see that. What can I do?"

This country is not one mass, collective heart. It is made up of millions of individual hearts. Good and bad, soft and hard, willing and unwilling. I know them all. What you can do is turn your heart to me and let me open your eyes to see what you can do. I'm not asking for a major contribution or for you to paint placards and walk in a demonstration. I'm asking you to notice what people around you need. When you can meet that need, do it. If this nation became less interested in what it needed and more interested in what others needed, it would become a very powerful nation indeed.

"I'm sorry we're so selfish, that we've made our own needs and interests more important than everyone else's. I'm sorry we've closed our eyes to our neighbors and have refused to aid them as much as we should. I'm sorry for my individual contribution to this collective selfishness. Help me to look outside myself, to see the needs of others around me, and to recognize what I have to contribute. I'll need willingness to give rather than take, Father. Can you help me to tear my gaze from myself?"

Of course. All you have to do is look at *me*.

Day 20

✠

what in my community or nation brings you joy?

Whether you realize it or not, the community and nation in which you live has a redemptive purpose in this world. God has gifted them with unique roles in the big picture. When, as a community or nation, we connect with that God-given purpose, even a little, God rejoices.

In case you've had an overdose of bleak newscasts, let me remind you that God has not abandoned you as a community or nation any more than he has abandoned you as an individual. So what is he up to? Let's ask!

"Lord, what in my community or nation brings you joy today? We're so good at emphasizing the negative, but where are the bright spots? Why do these things bring you joy? How can I bless that? How can I get involved? Restore my hope in my community and my nation today as I see them through your eyes. Show me what you are up to, and I will rejoice with you."

what in my community or nation brings you joy?

Today, I'm really glad I'm the one asking the questions. I would find it nearly impossible to answer this question for a number of reasons. Mainly, I just don't know enough about the workings of this nation to give any sort of educated guess on the answer, and I find it hard to believe that we, as a country, have done anything lately that would produce any kind of joy for God. Pessimistic would best describe my heart as I look for God this morning.

I see the Lord standing on the large map again, right in the middle. He gestures for me to join him. He looks grim, contemplative, and I guess he's having as much trouble finding joy in this place as I am.

"Father, is there anything in this nation that brings you joy?"

You don't have much faith that I can find joy here, do you?

"No, I feel a little pessimistic this morning. Actually, I wanted to avoid this question altogether. I struggled to get out of bed to ask you about this."

I know. But I do want to answer it. I *have* found joy here, and I want you to find it, too.

"Show me, then. My eyes can't see it."

That's because you're focusing on the wrong things. You're looking at this country as a whole, as a big wheel that's constantly turning, and often not in the direction you think is wise. You're equating this nation with a building,

a government, a group of people who have been given the task to run this nation and its affairs. No wonder you feel pessimistic; you've put your hope in man.

"Then where do I look? On what should I focus?"

Do you want to see what I see?

"Yes."

Suddenly, tiny pinpricks of light start to appear all over the map on which Jesus and I are standing. From the extreme east to the far west, from the remote north to the border in the south, tiny lights keep coming on. I'm fascinated by their presence and even more so by the sheer number of them.

"What do those lights represent?" I ask, already suspecting I know the answer.

The lights represent hearts that are turned toward me. You only see the blackness, the godlessness, the country that no longer calls itself 'Christian.' But I can see the hearts of the people of this nation that have turned fully toward me. That brings me joy. Look at all the lights that cover this map. Of course, there could be more, but how can I not be joyful about what I see here? These people make a difference in this nation. They wave my banner. They belong to *my* nation first and foremost, and that brings me joy.

The lights are dazzling. There are literally millions. I had no clue there were so many or that those tiny lights could light up such a large area so brilliantly. I feel joy welling up as I look at the lights flickering on the map. There are even lights, lots of them, that shine from those buildings, that government, those people that have been given the task of running this nation. The feeling of joy is now accompanied by hope as I survey my country through the eyes of my Father.

Day 21

✠

What is the Best use of my Day?

I hope that by now you are beginning to get a feel for the joys and sorrows in the heart of God. This is the beginning of true friendship with the Lord.

Now we want to shift gears and pose a series of questions that address the day at hand. We often pre-schedule our days completely, such that God's agenda is either excluded or regarded as an interruption. Too often we're like the priest and the Levite in the parable of the Good Samaritan (Luke 10:30-37) who were too busy to see that God had inserted a "divine appointment" into their day. We need to carve out space for the spontaneous in our lives lest we settle for rushing along and missing God's preordained adventures.

You can begin on this course by asking God, "What is the best use of my day?" before your head even leaves the pillow. God may be very specific or he may just give you a general "heads-up" on what to watch for. So let's ask!

what is the Best use of my Day?

"Father, I confess that I find this question threatening sometimes. I usually have my schedule all worked out. I know where and when I need to be in certain places, and I'm afraid that if I ask you about it, well, you might just throw me a curve ball that I'm not ready for. Of course, I should know by now that when you insert something into my day, I usually end up viewing it as a highlight rather than a hindrance. Still, I hesitate. However, I still need to ask, and so I'll look for you now.

"Jesus? Where can we meet this morning?"

I see him in my heart's yard, swinging in the redemption swing. I run to that place in my heart and throw my arms around him. My heart swells with love for him as we embrace. He is so good to me! Without releasing my grasp, I speak, my chin resting on his shoulder.

"Good morning, Jesus. I'm so glad we're together first thing this morning. You've made my day already, and it hasn't even really started."

I let go, only to find his eyes, and I am overwhelmed with the love that pours out of them. Suddenly, I'm in the story of Mary and Martha, and *I know* why Mary was unable to leave Jesus' side. If he told me that the best use of my day was to stay right where I am, I would not be disappointed. He's so close I think I might have just felt his breath on me.

"What's the best use of my day today, Jesus?"

He laughs out loud and rubs his hands together.

You are going to have a great day! My only request is that you take me along. I want to be there and see all that unravels today, to cheer with you, to enjoy every little thing that you discover. I want to be part of the day. I know I see all that's happening with you anyway, but I long to be *invited*. I want you to notice my presence as you walk through your day, not only in hindsight but right in the moment when I show my glory. I want to see your eyes light up when you see me, when our eyes meet.

"Well, if you're looking for an official invitation, here it is: Jesus, I would be honored if you would join me on my adventure today. Whatever comes my way, I want you to be at my side. I want you to join me in laughing or crying, whatever comes. If there's time to play, then play with me. If I'm to face pain, then face it with me, please. If there are divine appointments I don't know about yet, please help me to be in the right place at the right time. I need you to join me today. Will you?"

I'm not going anywhere without you. Thank you for the invitation!

Day 22

✠

Where Do You Want to Meet Me Today?

If Jesus is with us all the time, why bother asking him where he'd like to meet? We ask this question to remind ourselves to always be aware of God's presence. God's answer may relate to our inner life of prayer or to the outer realm of daily life. It all depends on the day we are about to have.

I like to ask Jesus this question whenever I sit down to pray. The Lord always responds by painting inner pictures in which I can behold him. You experienced this when you asked God to show you your heart. But you don't have to restrict yourself to that image. There is no end of inner landscapes he will create as meeting places.

On the other hand, I encourage you to ask God where the two of you can rendezvous today in the realm of your physical world. Take note of the anticipation you feel in actually going somewhere to meet with him. When you arrive there, ask God, "Why here?" Enjoy some time together on this special date.

where do you want to meet me today?

I love this question! I ask it all the time. For years, I tried to clear my mind when I went into prayer, trying to capture every thought and just leave a blank space in which to meet God. Needless to say, my prayer life was frustrating and distracted. When I learned to meet Jesus in a location, my prayer times were revolutionized. Having a meeting place draws all of my focus to that location and to God within it. Rather than battling to keep my mind blank, it is now fully engaged in what God is saying and doing so there is little room left for distraction.

"Jesus, as I start my day, I want to know where you want to meet with me."

When I take time to ask this first thing in the morning, I'm always pleasantly surprised by that day's turn of events. It feels like I'm better able to handle the unexpected, because I'm more aware of where he is.

I see Jesus sitting beside me in our van. It looks like we will spend the day together doing all the things I'm anticipating.

"Is there anything you want to do today?" I ask.

I just want to experience the day with you, that's all. I like it when we drive together, when we chit chat while you do your errands. I like it when you include me in the little things, not just the big requests. I feel more like your friend when we share life together rather than just having formal meetings.

It was like that for me with the disciples. We spent our days together for three years. We didn't have to store up the experiences of our day to share with each other later on. We lived those experiences together. They became our history, our memories.

I want that same kind of relationship with you. I don't want to hear merely what you did at the end of the day, I want to walk through the entire day with you and be part of the memory!

"That's what I want, too."

We head off together, with my to-do list in hand. I realize I want to take him everywhere with me, into every activity and encounter I experience this day.

Day 23

✠

Where will I see you today?

Whenever I present this question to God, I am making a choice to be alert throughout the entire day. I am daring the Lord to show himself once again in this earthly realm. He may use my devotional time to warn me where to look or he may just prepare a surprise for me later on.

Where will I notice him? Will he peek out at me through the glories of the natural world, stunning me with a snowy mountain landscape or hinting of his care through the busy mothering of our local wrens? Will I see him in the eyes of a stranger begging on the street corner or hear him laugh with the children on the playground?

When I ask this question, I realize it's actually God who is issuing the challenge: "Will you see me today? Will you notice if I tap you on the shoulder or look you in the eye?"

"O Lord, open my eyes to see you today!"

where will i see you today?

"Father, this question just begs you to show off. There is no end to how you can answer it. It's always a wonderful treat to see how you will do it! Your entire creation bears your signature. But like any beautiful painting, I need to pause to recognize the artist. At times, I have overlooked you in my daily comings and goings. I have been unable to see your signature on the face of a baby or in the hug of a friend. But when I ask, when I really want to see you, that's when you pull out the fireworks.

"Today, I see your face in the mountains that surround us here in the Fraser Valley. They constantly point their peaks at the One who created them. They wear different garments according to the seasons. And just when I think I've seen the most beautiful of those garments, you clothe them anew, and my breath escapes my lips in praise of the Creator.

"Father, Creator of this stunning part of the world, I know this question is more for me than for you. You've made yourself plain to see throughout this world. But I ask you to remove the scales from my eyes. Help me to see you even more clearly."

When I am done speaking, Jesus stands before me and grins with a full set of teeth. I realize that, just like me, he wants to be noticed and recognized, too. He's ready to show himself to anyone who asks, and he's always pleased to do it.

Today I will be everywhere! You'll see me in the mountains,

in the snow, in the lights of the city, and in the structures that rise up around you. You'll see me in your children and in your husband. You will bump into me every time you go out walking down the street. Don't assume I'll be in the obvious; I love to hide in unexpected people and places. This is my world, I know it well, and I shine in and through it. Don't blink, because you may just miss a glimpse of me!

I look around, bright-eyed and ready to see Jesus peek out at me. I love the feeling of recognizing him in a crowd or in a beautiful setting. My heart jumps inside me as I realize the privilege my God has afforded me. He isn't far away. He isn't aloof or distant. He is here, beside me, waiting for my eyes to meet his. And when we do meet and I see him shining out at me, my heart is set right. I am reassured that he is still God, still in control, and still willing to love me and show himself to me.

Day 24

✠

what promise do you have for me today?

In Hebrews 11 (often dubbed "the faith chapter"), we learn the heroes of faith were those who received a promise from God and then believed it. But when they listened to God, they heard promises that required more than a nod. Their belief was an active trust that they obeyed even to the point of death.

When you ask God for a promise, you can count on him to give one. But the ball is very quickly back in your court. Will you believe him? What if he really means it? What response does that demand from you? Will it change how you live today?

A friend recently made a New Year's resolution to take up running. But then the Lord spoke to him, saying, "I am making a resolution, too. Whenever you call on me, I will always come running to you. And by the way: I always keep my resolutions."

With this in mind, do you dare the ask the question: "Lord, what promise do you have for me today?"

what promise do you have for me today?

"Father, I believe you have a promise for me today. But I'm not so sure I can receive it. I don't want to hurt you or grieve you by saying that. I just need to find you and ask a few questions before I ask for my promise.

"Father, this question really tests my faith. I know you are true to your word—I have no doubt about that. But a promise has to be both given and received. My testing comes in having the faith to receive your promise. I self-impose a list of questions whenever you give me a promise. They seem designed to undermine the gift in the promise. So, as I ask this question, I know you are up to something in my heart."

In response, Jesus shows me my heart's yard. It has become such a familiar place for me these days. I feel comfortable here even though it's still in a state of excavation. We find that redemption swing, that sweet patch of green grass from which we can survey the rest of my heart. As we sit down together on the swing, I realize I'm trembling.

What's the matter?

"I think I'm scared."

What's scaring you?

"Disappointment," I reply. As soon as the word forms in my mind, it brings fear to my heart. It's disappointment that prevents me from moving forward, from embracing the promises I have been given and from asking for more. Despair creeps in and threatens to rob me of my precious time with the Father. Thankfully, Jesus steps in.

Eden, let me fight this battle for you. Let me remove this despair from your heart and replace it with hope.

"Gladly, but how is that possible?"

I promise not to disappoint you!

Those words, that promise, cut into the despair like a knife. But can one promise defeat my enemy? I look into Jesus' eyes wanting to see something that will tell me the battle is over and that hope can reign in my heart once again. I take his wonderful face in my hands and search his eyes. Suddenly, I see it: love. He loves me, he cares about my heart, and he longs to meet my needs. *That* love can defeat my despair and conquer my fear of disappointment!

My trembling stops. I lean in to Jesus' shoulder and relax in the strength of his embrace. The despair lifts, and a new thing bubbles up from deep within my heart. I think it's hope. I look back up into those loving eyes.

I promise not to disappoint you!

All at once, I believe him.

Day 25

✠

who can i encourage today?

What a remarkably simple question! Does the Bible ever tell us God expects us to encourage others? Of course! Yet often it doesn't occur to us that God has prepared people for us to bless today, and on purpose at that!

We can always be encouraging in a general way, but why not push it further? Ask God to show you someone specific who needs encouragement. Ask him why that person needs encouragement. Does he have a promise for you to deliver? A gift? An act of kindness? How would he like you to deliver it? A letter, a phone call, or in person? What "love language" does he want you to use? Is there a Scripture he'd like you to share with that person? Or perhaps just a gift of time spent together.

Just watch: When you give God space to lead you in the ministry of encouragement, he will elevate your words and acts into a truly prophetic gift. Will you invite him to do that today?

who can i encourage today?

I have been amazed for years by the God-given power of encouragement. There's something addictive about using it to strengthen others. I love watching the words sink into their heart. Afterwards, I enjoy watching them stand a little taller, hold their head a little higher. And I love the sparkle in their eyes; the way encouragement seems to feed each heart and restore things within them that may have been lost.

"So, who should I encourage today, Jesus?" I ask.

He stands beside me as I look out my hotel room window. The city spreads out in all directions beneath me as I view it from fifteen stories above. My mind marvels at the number of people my eyes can see never mind all of the people hidden inside the buildings and homes around me. Where can I possibly begin in my quest to encourage others? Almost as soon as the question forms in my mind, Jesus speaks.

I want you to begin at home.

My heart sighs with that good news. I get to encourage Brad and the boys today! It's probably been a while since I went out of my way to encourage them. I love them and tell them so all the time, but encouragement is different than saying, "I love you." It's taking time to notice something specific to highlight about each of them. Words might do the trick for one of the boys. But the other one needs touch, and Brad will want a listening ear. Sometimes encouragement is best given by posting the drawing that took so much time and effort on the front of the fridge. I wonder what Jesus has in mind today.

"Is there anything in particular that you want me to say or do?"

Yes. I want you to be intentional. I want you to take the time to find what each one really needs to hear or feel. I think you've got a pretty good idea for each of them, but take your time today, enjoy the process of wrapping up your gift to them.

"I think I'm going to enjoy this."

Yes, you're meant to.

Day 26

✠

whose Burdens do i carry? will you take them?

Are you a "burden-bearer"? Scripture tells us that bearing the burdens of others fulfills Christ's law of love (Galatians 6:2). It's good to help others carry their burdens—as long as you remember you don't have to do it forever. There's a destination where all burdens must be set down: the Cross.

Empathizing with those in need is a godly trait, but it can become a heavy yoke rather quickly. In fact, if we cling to these burdens ourselves, we run the danger of becoming mini-messiahs, trying to fix circumstances and control the lives of others. We ought to love one another, but let's leave the job of Saviour to Jesus alone. You'll find that the act of handing those who need grace over to God is a powerful act of intercession. As you release them to God, he releases grace to them.

Today, ask God whose burden you can bring to him. How does he see them? How does he see their burden? What promise does he have for them?

whose burdens do i carry? will you take them?

My heart wants to caution me about this question. It wants to tell me that carrying others' burdens to Jesus is heavy and awkward, and it's too difficult to put them down. But I want to ask Jesus about this, I want to know what he wants to do.

"Jesus, where can we meet today?"

I find myself standing outside my childhood home. This house and property has been "home" since I was a toddler. After 38 years of living at this corner of the world, my parents have sold and are moving at the end of this month. I've seen the burden they carry over this. They have to pack up, sell, give away, and otherwise bring some sort of end to 38 years of memories and "stuff."

"Jesus, what can I carry for them?" I ask. "What can I bring to you that will lighten their load?"

Bring me their hearts.

I see my dad standing in his big shed surrounded by all those tools, gadgets, and little inventions he's created to make his gardening and yard work easier over the years. I see the burden of packing all of this up on his back. It's so heavy it threatens to crush him.

I see my mom in her kitchen, the one she designed and dreamed of for years. Her burden is twofold: she carries her own over responsibility for this move, and then, in addition, carries my dad's burden as well. I can see these burdens are far too heavy for either of them.

114

"How do I bring you their hearts?" I ask.

Grab them by their hands and bring them to me.

I take them both by the hand and pull them gently toward Jesus. The three of us stand before him, and, all at once, I notice how able he seems to take on their burdens.

"Jesus, can we take these burdens off my mom and dad? You can see they're being crushed by the weight of them. Can I take them off?"

Go ahead.

I reach for my mom's first, and I'm surprised to discover the burden is much heavier than it looked. She's a strong woman, but this is way too much. I actually have to drag the burden to Jesus' feet. As I drag it, I feel what the burden was to my mom. When I finally reach Jesus, I rest the burden at his feet and head back for my dad's. His burden looks like an oversized tool belt. When I lift it off him, it also drops to the ground, and I have to drag it to Jesus' feet as well.

Let those burdens rest here, Eden. Now bring me their hearts.

I do the only thing I can think of. I pick up each of them, as if they were young children, and deposit their entire beings into Jesus' arms.

Can you let them rest here with me?

I realize this is the test. Can I leave them and their burdens with Jesus?

You know I'm able.

"More than me and more than them."

Then let *me* carry them.

As I back away, I see peace in my parents' eyes. I look again, and their burdens are gone!

Day 27

✠

who have i judged?
how do you see them?

This question is meant to heal our eyes of the judgements we make about others. Isaiah predicted Jesus would never judge according to what his eyes saw but rather by listening to the Holy Spirit (Isaiah 11:1-4). Jesus himself exhorted us frequently not to judge others at all, especially not according to their outward appearance. Yet even the most careful person can slip into all sorts of prejudice—racism, sexism, ageism, and so forth. Even when such judgements are accurate, they are spiritually illegal. God alone sits as judge of the living and the dead. How can we be freed from this habit? God offers a solution. He wants to lend us his eyes.

Today, start by asking God the following question: "Lord, is there a person or people whom I have judged? I confess to sitting in your judgement seat on more than one occasion. I relinquish it now. Instead, would you please lend me your eyes? How shall I see these people? How shall I treat them? I welcome your attitude toward them in my heart."

who have i judged?
how do you see them?

I've been busy for some time examining my heart to find someone whom I have judged and not taken to Jesus. I've been unable to come up with someone, so I know that's my cue to ask Jesus for help. I'm not naïve enough to think my heart is that pure. Sometimes I'm just that blind.

"Jesus can we meet somewhere *really* safe today? If we're going to be looking into my heart that closely, I want to feel secure."

Where do you feel the safest?

"Right beside you," I reply immediately, realizing that the location doesn't make a situation safe, *he* does.

Then come close and let me hold you while we take a look at your heart.

I tuck in close to his side, and he embraces me as he waits patiently for me to begin.

"I can't seem to come up with a name or see the face of a person I've judged and not already taken care of. I know my heart isn't that pure. Can you help me by showing me who I've judged?"

Suddenly, there she is, and I realize that while I've taken her to Jesus numerous times, I still have judgments that stick out of her body like arrows. These wounds cover her body, and I wince at the magnitude of the damage my little arrows of judgment have managed to inflict.

"I'm sorry my judgment has caused her so much wounding. You know I've taken her to you many times before. What else can I do? How can I stop shooting more arrows her way?"

It would help if you gave your bow to me.

"My bow?"

Your bow is your *desire* to judge. As long as you still have the desire, you will find the arrows to shoot from it. The arrows lay all around you. Every time you perceive something you don't like about a person, you have the choice of whether or not to pick up the arrow at your feet. But if you've given me the bow, the desire to judge, then the arrow really becomes quite useless.

Suddenly, I can see the bow in my hands. It's covered with blood. I hold it out toward Jesus. "This bow is covered in blood, Jesus. I want you to have it."

Jesus takes it from my hands.

"Can you show me something about her besides the things I don't like? Can you show me how you see her?"

I see her as a little girl that doesn't know I love her. She's heard the words but has never felt my love. The very things she does that bother you the most are her attempts to feel my love.

"Those arrows I've shot at her, do they prevent her from feeling your love?"

Have you ever tried to hug someone with an arrow in them?

119

It's too painful for them to receive. It only drives the arrow deeper.

"Then can we *please* remove these arrows now? I really do want her to feel your love."

We move toward her. As I get closer, I see that each arrow has something written on it. The words are my silent judgments, and they have embedded themselves deep into her heart. Tears fill my eyes as I understand the gravity of my sin and the pain I have inflicted.

"Please forgive me for judging her, Jesus."

Done.

"Thank you for showing me mercy. Can I ask one more thing? Could you bring some relief to her wounds, especially the ones for which I am responsible?

I can and I will.

Day 28

✠

against whom do i hold hard feelings?

Following up the question about judgments, we had planned to ask, "Is there anyone I need to forgive?" But I suspected it would be too easy to evade God's answer. Asking if I am carrying "hard feelings" seems to bring things into sharper focus. For example, I may have spoken words of forgiveness to those who've offended me. But I might find that I continue to labor under feelings that are "hard" on me—and that person. Thus, when I state the question this way, I open my heart to deeper cleansing and healing.

We can release people who have offended us to the Lord in the same way we handed over those for whom we felt burdened.

We begin by asking, "Do I have hard feelings toward anyone? Is there resentment or bitterness in my heart that I need to confess? Do I need to approach this person, or is it between you and me? How do you see that person? Are there wounds in my heart that you still want to heal?"

against whom do i
hold hard feelings?

My heart is feeling rather vulnerable being under the microscope like this. It feels like it's had a good going over, and yet there's still so much more to examine. It could be that I want to avoid facing the fact that there may still be ungodly feelings within, even after all this soul searching. I don't trust myself to do this alone. I need Jesus to help me.

"Jesus, I need you here. I want to feel safe."

He comes again, so dependable, so sweet to be my friend, so willing to walk through all of this with me and keep me safe. His eyes are so clear they settle the fear in my heart immediately. I wonder if there will ever be a time when all of my feelings are in his control.

We sit down together on a comfortable couch, and he rests his arm around me. I couldn't feel safer.

"I need you to help me answer this question: Is there anyone I have hard feelings toward?"

Let me help you see it yourself. Is there anyone you would rather not bump into in a store? Or is there anyone you would avoid if at all possible? Is there someone who, when you see him or her, causes you to clench your teeth and force yourself to be nice?

"When you put it that way, I can see a couple of people. But does that mean I have hard feelings toward them?"

Well, what's happening in your heart when you see them?

"I cringe inside."

Why?

"Because I don't feel like they're 'for me.' I don't trust who they are or what they will say about our meeting afterwards. So I cringe, because I feel like I have to be so careful."

Do you like that feeling?

"No."

Is it hard?

"Yes."

Then there's your answer. You have hard feelings toward them.

"What can I do about it? How can I soften my feelings toward them?"

Use my eyes to see them. Ask me to be there with you right at that moment. Let me show you what you need to see in them that will soften your heart for them.

"Do I have to wait until I see them next?"

No, we can meet them right now if you'd like. Do you want to bring them to your heart?

"Yes, I would. I don't want to wait to clean this up."

Can you see them?

"They're coming toward me. Can you show me what you see,

Jesus?"

What I see next is stunning. They both carry chisels, and they are heading straight for my heart. When I look at my heart, I see a small part that has become hard, like stone. They come to my heart and, with their chisels, begin to chip away at that hard part. I turn suddenly to face Jesus.

"You're behind this! You're using them to chip away these hard feelings. But wouldn't a softer touch be better?"

Have you ever broken a stone with a sponge or a cloth? You need something hard to break something hard.

I look back at their faces now, and I see Jesus in them. He's smiling out at me from within them, and I know that he's "for me." My hard feelings are beginning to soften, because I'm seeing Jesus, not the chisels. I relax, knowing now that my heart will be well taken care of.

Day 29

✠

Is anything hindering our friendship?

Is anything hindering your friendship with God? Don't be too hasty to answer lest you slip into presumption on the one hand or self-condemnation on the other. In other words, don't try to figure it out on your own. ASK!

True, Paul tells the Corinthians to examine themselves, but only after he's already admitted in 1 Corinthians 14:3 that he doesn't even judge himself. God has to make those calls. Don't worry: We aren't trying to fabricate another "hoop" for you to jump through with this exercise. We're simply keeping the friendship growing and the channels clear and open.

When I ask God this question, he often shows me that sin is NOT the primary hindrance to our friendship. Sometimes he shows me that my *politeness* can stifle the relationship. If I'm repressing my true feelings, I am not truly "looking him in the eye." He needs me to be brutally honest if we're going to go deeper together. With that in mind, let's pose the question: "Lord, is there anything hindering our friendship? Is anything stalling our intimacy? Please show me."

is anything hindering our friendship?

This question makes me smile. I have no idea what the answer will be, but I smile because I know that Jesus is my friend! He's not someone that I'm just friendly with or that I know enough about to chit chat with. He is my true friend. I have shared my heart openly with him and, in turn, he has embraced me and all of my weaknesses. My friendship with him has changed my heart, and so I trust that if there is something that hinders me from being even closer to him, I need to know what it is, and I need to hear it directly from him.

"Jesus, my friend, where will we meet today?"

Instantly, we're back in the coffee shop sharing some hot drinks and enjoying this oasis of friendship. My heart is full, and tears trickle down my face as I take in the magnitude of the privilege I have in calling Jesus "friend."

"I want you to know that if our friendship never went any deeper, I would still be fully satisfied."

I hear what you're saying, but I can't say the same. I want a deeper relationship with you, Eden. As much as I've enjoyed the depth of friendship we have, I still want more. I long to visit every corner of your heart, to look under every rock, behind every tree, and to experience all that is before you! We've really only scratched the surface. There is so much more for us to explore together!

"Is there anything that hinders you and I from doing that?"

Only your fears of being known. You've come so far, but there is so much more I want you to reveal to me. I see you cringe at that, but you need to know that being known, especially by me and yourself, is what will make our friendship so much sweeter. The more we discover about your heart, the more treasure we find, the more garbage we can remove, and the more space there is for *us*.

"I want to be brave enough to go to all the corners of my heart, but I'm afraid of what might be hidden there. What if we discover something that would make you turn away from me? What if..."

Don't ask "What if..." questions. There's nothing that can make me turn away from you. There's nothing we can discover that will surprise me. Remember, I'm God. It's really you that's doing the discovering. You're just letting me join you. I've known your heart all along. Our friendship is about you discovering what I already know about your heart.

"So you know my heart and you still want to be my friend?"

It's because I know your heart that I can't help but want to be your friend.

If all of this is true, then I have no need to fear being known. He already knows me, absolutely, completely, fully. If he hasn't turned away yet, he's never going to!

"Jesus, I love you! Your friendship is my life. Thank you for knowing me, loving me, and being my friend!"

Day 30

✠

What Burdens Will You Bear for Me?

Are you carrying any burdens? Earlier, we referred to bearing others' burdens to the Cross. Now we must attend to our own burdens. Burdens of worry, guilt or grief are just a few examples of the things we tend to pack around. You might even feel them physically in your shoulders and neck. What does Jesus say about this? In Matthew 11, he makes us an offer: "Come. That load has become too heavy, and you've become so tired. Give it to me, and I will exchange it for some good soul-rest" (my paraphrase).

Today, ask the Lord if you are carrying a burden. Ask him to name it for you and to show you what it looks like to him. Ask him what it has cost you to carry this burden on your own. And ask him if you believe any lies that prevent you from handing it over to him. Finally, ask him what he would like to give you in exchange, and then tell him you are willing to make that trade. Invite him to take your burden and then receive his gift.

what Burdens will you Bear for me?

I can feel the weight of a burden on my shoulders and back. My muscles ache with the tension of trying to balance it as I walk. I stretch to try and eliminate the ache, but nothing short of having this burden removed will bring me relief. This is no illusion; I feel the weight of this spiritual burden throughout my entire being.

I need to bring my burden to Jesus, to have him lift it off and then leave it behind for him to carry. It's simple to say, but I find it quite difficult to do.

"Jesus, I need your help again today. Where can we meet?"

Don't move. I can see that you're straining under your load. I'll come to you.

I sigh with relief. "Thank you for having compassion on me even when I'm taking on what isn't mine to carry."

What have you got there?

"It's this book I'm writing. It feels like a weight on my back. I feel so responsible to do things right. I can rationalize that I can't attain perfection, but my heart still strives for it. The weight of this quest for perfection threatens to crush me, and it threatens to crush the book, too."

So are you prepared to pay that price?

"Can you show me exactly what the cost is?"

From what I see, it has cost you your back. It's also cost you some peace; peace I gave you to enjoy while writing this book. You traded my peace for a big bag of discomfort. It's also cost you some good sleep, because you were busy trying to figure things out instead of letting me tell you what needed to be done. It cost you some joy today, because when you should have been enjoying a great moment, you were thinking about what had to be done. Are you still prepared to pay for that?

"I can't afford it! The cost is way too high."

Can you see any reason why you couldn't just hand it over to me right now?

"Well, it does have an awful lot of my heart in it. I feel quite vulnerable handing it off."

I guess you'll have to trust me with it, won't you? Can you do that?

"I really want to, but it's like I'm carrying my heart on my back."

So you feel safer carrying your heart on your own back than you do giving it to me?

"Well, when you put it that way... It doesn't seem so safe."

It never was safe. I'm the only safe place to bring that burden—your book—and your heart. I want to carry it for you; it really would be my privilege to keep it safe for you. Will you let me do it?

I slip the straps of this burden off my shoulders like a backpack. The relief my muscles feel is immediate and overwhelming. As I look down at the burden, it's clear that the cost of carrying it was way too high. Any fool can see that now. I turn back to Jesus.

"It's yours, Jesus. I'm just not strong enough to carry it. I don't have what it takes to pay the bill."

Jesus picks up what was crushing me with surprising ease. Then he puts my heart on his back, and I know that it's finally safe!

Day 31

✠

What lies will you dispel for me?

Ever since Christ defeated Satan at the Cross, the only leverage the enemy still maintains against us is lies. What drives every form of fear (worry, anxiety, panic, insecurity, timidity, and so on)? What generates shame, worthlessness, hopelessness, and despair? Where do temptations, compulsions, and obsessions get their power to trip us up? In each of these cases, you will always find the same pathogen undermining our faith and draining us of life: a lie.

The fantastic news is that for every lie there exists a corresponding truth. This truth comes straight from the mouth of God like a sharp, two-edged sword. That's why merely facing and overcoming our lies is not enough. We must ask God to identify them and answer them with his truth. It is through this process that "the truth sets you free."

So take time today to ask God the following: "Lord, show me the lies that continue to trip me up. What liberating truth will set me free?"

what lies will
you dispel for me?

I think I have pretty good discernment. When our boys are not being completely truthful, I'm quick to see it in their faces and hear it in their voices. Even out in the world, I can sense the twisting of a lie quite easily. So why is it so hard for me to discern lies spoken against me? Initially, I can cast such lies aside. But they have a nasty habit of creeping back to accuse me again. And each time they do, I begin to believe just a bit of each lie, then a bit more until I have fully embraced the lie and succumbed to the power of its deception.

There is one lie that I have battled most of my adult life, and today, I think I'd like to put an end its power over me for good.

"Jesus, I need you. Can you bring your sword of truth?"

I see him come toward me. Not only is he carrying the sword of truth, he is completely dressed for battle.

"Is it that serious Jesus?"

More serious than you think, Eden. I want to kill this lie and not leave even a bit of it to come back and haunt you. It has had way too much power over you, and I want to destroy it for good.

The lie that I wear, that I've owned, that I've bowed to for years, is this: "I'm not worth it." Jesus addressed this lie in my heart several months ago, but at the time I was unable to give it over fully to Jesus so he could finish it off. In the time since I discovered that lie in my heart, Jesus has been countering that lie with his truth. I have begun to see the value he places on me, but that lie still remains rooted in my heart. I'm feeling braver today though. So perhaps for the first time, I'll smell freedom.

"Show me what it looks like, Jesus."

He does, and I'm horrified by what I see. I am draped in rags. They're filthy and smelly, and they hang off of me like torn sails on a deserted ship. I weep at the sight of what I have believed.

"Jesus, help me; I don't want this."

Can I take those rags from you?

As I nod my consent, he pulls out his sword. With each stroke of the sword, he speaks truth, and a piece of rag falls to the ground.

You are fearfully and wonderfully made!

Swipe. A piece of rag falls.

***My* works are marvelous!**

Swipe.

I watched you being formed and waited in expectation!

Swipe.

I loved you before the foundations of the earth.

Swipe.

I have written your name in my Book of Life.

Swipe.

You are precious to me. I value our friendship and want you to stand in my truth.

Swipe.

I look down at the rags that cover my feet and struggle not to pick them back up again to cover my nakedness. Before I give in to the power of the lie again, Jesus puts his hand under my chin and raises my eyes to his.

Let me clothe you, Eden.

He pulls out a garment unlike anything I have ever worn or seen and covers me with it. It is perfect in every way. Even a wonderful aroma oozes out from its fabric. Could this really be for me?

I am clothing you in my righteousness. There is no garment more precious than this! Wear my righteousness, and you will know your worth.

I bend down to pick up the rags and then hand them to Jesus.

"Will you take care of these?"

Absolutely!

Day 32

✠

are you with me always?
what does that mean?

My favorite promises from Scripture relate to the fact that God will never leave us or forsake us. Hebrews 13:5 actually contains a six-fold negative in the Greek. My son Dominic has memorized it quite literally as "I will NEVER, never, never, never, never, never leave you." We can rattle off such phrases rather quickly, but we can lose our sense of God's presence just as quickly. Would you like to be consciously aware that God is with you every hour of the day and night? David said, "I have set the LORD always before me. Because he is at my right hand, I will not be shaken" (Psalm 16:8).

What if you knew that God was just as near when you are struggling as when you are excelling? What if you knew that he wouldn't leave even when you are cranky or unfaithful? What would that do inside of you? How would it affect your lifestyle? Rather than supposing, let's just ask.

"Lord, I want to know: Is it true that you really are with me at all times? Would you give me assurance of your nearness today? What will that mean for me?"

are you with me always?
what does that mean?

I've never been more certain of God's answer to one of my questions, and yet for some reason, I have struggled to hear and write out this answer. It's not that I can't feel Jesus right beside me even now, but there is something else twisting at my heart this morning.

"Jesus? Where can we meet?"

Let's go for a walk today.

"Where will we go?"

Follow me.

He grabs my hand, tucks it under his arm, and we begin our walk. I can't prevent a smile from breaking out on my face. I am overwhelmed with the privilege of walking with Jesus, but I'm still hesitant to ask my question. We walk on for a long time in beautiful silence, but my heart continues to twist inside of me.

Do you have a question for me, Eden?

Jesus always knows when I need a bit of gentle prodding. "I do, but I don't want to ask it. I suspect I know the answer, and I'm curious about how you would answer it, but something in my heart is twisting. This doesn't feel good!"

What is it?

I take a moment to collect my thoughts and feelings. Suddenly, it's all there. I know what the problem is.

"What I'm feeling uncomfortable about is how I would answer this question if you were asking me. I couldn't possibly be as absolute as you in my answer. I know there have been many times when I haven't been with you, maybe even fully just walked away from you. So how can I ask if you're with me always if I can't be totally committed to being with you?"

Wow. You're kind of hard on yourself, don't you think? Remember which one of us is God here. I *do* want you with me, but I'm also very aware of your limits. I don't *need* you to be with me like you need me to be with you. I'm the constant here. I'm the one who is with you always.

I have been set straight, and his truth straightens the twisting in my heart.

Ask me, please. I want to answer.

"Okay, are you with me?"

Always!

"What does that mean?"

It means that my love is unconditional. My presence with you isn't subject to the conditions this world tries to put on you. No matter what, no matter where, I am with you. You can't run and hide; there is nowhere you can go that I won't be with you. There is nothing anyone else can do that can separate me from you. Are you getting the picture?

"Loud and clear."

How does that make you feel?

"Confident, like I'm not alone, like I could tackle almost anything."

Good, because there will be some things to tackle this year. But I'm not asking you to tackle them yourself. Remember, I'm with you always. This is the truth I want you to stand in this year: *I am with you always!*

"You honor me with your presence, Jesus. I want to stand in this truth, come what may."

Day 33

✠

will you guide me?
where are we heading?

"For this God is our God forever and ever; he will be our guide even to the end" (Psalm 48:14).

Here we have another promise from God's Word; a promise we'd like to appropriate afresh. Considering his offer to be our Wonderful Counselor, we likely don't ask God for advice often enough. Life is a complex journey, sometimes even a minefield. Yet we're told that we have a reliable Guide who is willing to lead the way. We need to remember to ask for his help, tune in to his voice, and then act on it no matter what.

Usually, God leads only a step or two at a time, but it doesn't hurt to check in regularly. Ask, "If you are guiding me, where are we heading?" Jesus tells us in John 16:13 that the Holy Spirit, the Counselor he promised to send us, will guide us into all truth, even revealing what is coming in the future. Your life is going somewhere. Today, ask if he'll show you something about where that future lies.

will you guide me?
where are we heading?

I have walked aimlessly for years, although I don't think those around me have really noticed it. I would shoot my arrows in any direction, not seeing a target for any one of them. I can't blame God for this. When I look back, he had clearly marked out the route. But I wasn't looking for markers. I thought that as long as I kept moving and looked busy, then I would eventually arrive somewhere. Right? Wrong. Busyness isn't synonymous with having a goal or direction. In fact, busyness can be the antipathy of focused, purposeful movement. I want my steps to be purposeful. I want to have a compass that God has set and a direction to follow.

"Father, where can we meet?"

We stand together on the bow of a small boat. Crystal blue water stretches out on all sides. There is no land in sight. The wind whips our hair, and the smell of salt tingles in our noses. The boat's motor has been shut off, the anchor dropped, and we rock in the calming rhythm of the waves.

"This is beautiful, Father."

Isn't it!

"I've got another question."

I know. Go ahead and ask.

"You know how I've stumbled around this world, looking busy and going nowhere? I need you to guide me. Will you?"

I would love to guide you! I have a plan. We won't drift aimlessly. I'm charting a course, and together, we are going to get there.

"Can you tell me where we're heading?"

I'm going to lead you closer to my heart.

"How do I get there?"

You follow me. It's important no to try and run ahead. As exciting as the destination may be, the process, the adventure of getting there, is just as exciting and, ultimately, just as important.

I feel a little dizzy with excitement. Questions begin to flood my thoughts. What will this look like? When will we start? How long will it take? Will I know when we get there?

"Can I ask when we'll be starting?"

A wonderful smile spreads across my Father's face. He stretches out his hand and points at the crystal sea.

You've already begun. We've left the land far behind.

I look around, stunned. "When did we start?"

The day you first invited me into your heart's yard. We can't dig into your heart without having your heart move closer to mine. Every time we take out something that doesn't belong in your heart, you move closer to mine. Every time we discover a gift or reclaim hidden treasure, you are moving closer to my heart. I have made your steps purposeful,

because you have let me guide you through your heart.

"How long will this journey take?"

As long as you have. We aren't going to take any shortcuts. The journey is far too precious to rush. Are you willing to continue?

I take a deep breath, like it's my first.

"I have no other desire but to journey closer to your heart. Lead on!"

Day 34

✠

What Dreams Do You Want to Awaken in Me?

Once we stop running our lives on our own and start asking God to take the lead, we may begin to see ourselves—mistakenly—as God's pawns, automatons without free will. Unfortunately, that thinking leads to the death of the very dreams and desires God wants us to pursue.

Psalm 37:4 tells us that as we delight in the Lord, he will give us the desires of our heart. Far from being selfish, many of our dreams are meant to be awakened, and God himself is willing to breathe life into them. Remember: It is the enemy—not God—who is the thief of dreams.

Today, come before the Lord and ask him if he would like to awaken a dream or desire that you had previously shelved or buried. As he reveals this to you, you might be tempted to laugh it off as grandiose or impractical. But ask the Lord what the first steps toward that dream look like, and then be willing to take them.

what dreams do you want to awaken in me?

I've read a number of books recently on the whole topic of dreams and desires. It's odd how I'm able to fan the flame for the dreams of others but have a difficult time even sparking my own. I know I have one big desire, and that's to have our own home. Beyond that, I dig around in my heart and seem to come up empty-handed. I hope Jesus knows where to dig today.

"Jesus?"

Yes.

"I can't seem to locate my dreams. Do I even have any?"

They're in there!

"When I dig around for them, I just come up empty-handed. Maybe I don't know what I'm looking for."

It's possible. Would you like some help?

"Yes, please." We walk from the edge of my heart's yard to a relatively untouched spot tucked between some monstrous piles of dirt. I've been to this area of my heart before, but I haven't visited it in a very long time. "So this is where my dreams are?" I ask, eyeing the ground skeptically.

If you let me dig.

"It sounds painful."

It could be. Will you let me dig *even* if it hurts?

I struggle to answer. How badly do I want to know what my dreams are? And when we find them, then what? Do dreams really come true? If not, I'd rather not unearth them. Won't my dreams merely become a source of pain if they aren't realized?

"Jesus, fear has crept into me today. Will you please calm my heart and throw out the fear that threatens to rob me of my dreams?"

Nothing **will be stolen today!**

With those words, fear slinks off, and the turmoil inside subsides. Jesus looks at me now with a questioning gaze.

Ready?

"All right."

I hear the familiar sound of the backhoe starting up. Jesus climbs into the cab and invites me to join him. Using the bucket, he cuts deep into my heart, like he expects to go to the very core, and maybe he does. I watch as each scoop cuts deeper and deeper. And yet what comes out is only soil, not dreams. Maybe I really *don't* have any dreams. Maybe Jesus doesn't know where to dig *either.*

Just then, in the last scoop, we spot something: a jar. Jesus swings the shovel gently to the side and deposits the jar on the ground without breaking it. He shuts down the backhoe, and we climb out of the cab and walk over to the jar.

"That was buried pretty deep," I remark.

Too deep!

I pick up the jar, brush off the dirt, and turn it over in my hands to get a better look at its contents. "It looks fragile." The jar is packed with ribbons of different colors and lengths. "These are my dreams?"

They're in there!

"What do I do with them now?"

Could we just look at them one at a time?

"That sounds good."

Jesus picks up the jar and unscrews the lid. He pulls out a long piece of yellow ribbon.

This is your dream about having your own home.

"But I knew that!"

Yes, but you've kept it under glass. I want to let it out!

"What about the other dreams?"

We'll get to them. We're going to pull them all out, don't worry.

As I watch the yellow ribbon flutter in the breeze, one end tucked safely in Jesus' hand, I realize I have to trust that he can do this with every ribbon—and dream—in that jar. I also realize this may take a while....

Day 35

✠

why is "it" like that? what can be done?

Do you ever wonder why things are the way they are? And have you ever been told not to ask such questions of God? Many Christians feel it's inappropriate to ask God "Why?" questions. I suspect that's because they don't believe he really wants to answer them. But I want to release you from such teachings.

Feel free to ask God "Why?" any time you want. Understand that God always reserves the right to say, "None of your business." But, as the apostle James says, "We have not, because we ask not" (James 4:2). This includes answers to every dilemma and mystery of life. Rather than avoid such issues, we need to develop a habit of looking to God for the root issues of life's quandaries instead of just moaning about the symptoms.

Take time today to ponder a situation that troubles you in your family, business, church or the broader world. Then ask, "Why is it like that?" or "Why did that happen?" Follow up with, "What can be done?" or "What do I need to know about that?"

why is "it" like that?
what can be done?

Brad and I have been in full-time ministry for fifteen years now. As I reflected on that this morning, I realized *that* is a long time! Definitely long enough to notice some things about how the church operates and to come up with some questions surrounding that. But rather than attempt to answer them on my own, I need to find Jesus, the Lover of the Bride, his church.

"Jesus, can we talk about your Bride?"

Of course.

"I know fifteen years is a blink of the eye to you, but for me it's a significant chunk of my life. I wanted to ask you about some of the things I've noticed about your Bride from my experience. I'm not on a fault-finding mission; I only want to see things with *your* understanding about why we, as the church, do certain things."

I'm listening.

"I'm convinced we all love you, or at least we've all fallen in love with one or more of your attributes. But why is it that we can't seem to get together? I don't mean becoming one big church, all believing the same things and following the same guidelines. I mean, why can't it feel like we're all on the same team? We have to work so hard at constantly building bridges between different churches. Why is that?"

Fear.

"Fear of what?"

Of nearly everything. One church is afraid of the other's doctrines. Another one is afraid of the other's gifts, and the list goes on. To control the fear, man has created smaller, more manageable brides. Instead of there being one glorious Bride, she has been segmented into parts. Her hands are over here, her feet over there, her heart in yet another place. Can you see that?

"Clearly! So is it too late? Or is there still something that can be done?"

It's *never* too late. I have the power to redeem, remember? That means there is *always* hope!

"So where do we go from here?"

Instead of finding a place away from everyone else, setting up a little camp and protecting it with flimsy walls of doctrine or styles of worship, do something radical. Move your tent pegs as close to the next tent as you can. Enjoy your neighbors, who are really your brothers and sisters. You'll hear their pots and pans rattle, and they'll hear yours. Sometimes you'll trip over each other's tent pegs, but you'll have grace for one another. And soon, more tents will arrive, because they will see that the community of the Bride is being built, and they'll want to become part of it.

"I love the Bride you're describing! She looks so healthy."

Just watch: She will be!

Day 36

✠

Where are you in this?
What are you doing?

To follow up the question of why things are as they are, we want to ask God where he is in these situations. He's not only present with you everywhere, always. He is also present and active in every type of situation you can imagine.

My good friend Brian West was visiting Disneyland a few years back. He paused to watch the busy crowds, the plethora of eye-catching amusements, and especially the awestruck children. It occurred to him to ask God, "Where are you in this? What are you doing here?" The Lord spoke to Brian about that, addressing both what grieved him and what brought him joy in that place.

Today, you can do the same thing no matter where you are. You can take the quandary you were discussing with God yesterday and ask, "So where are you in that? What are you up to?" Prepare to be truly amazed. Brian was.

where are you in this?
what are you doing?

I'll get straight to it: "So where are you in all of this, Jesus?"

Where I've always been, right here. I'm not afraid of who the Bride is. I've been at her side this entire time. I have no designs on leaving.

"Can you show these blind eyes exactly where you've been?"

I see the coffee shop we use as our church office. It's become a beehive of activity, usually hosting at least one table of people who call Fresh Wind their home. It's become a base for us, a regular place where we can be found by those who need us. I see Jesus walking from table to table, greeting and loving those who have come to be refreshed. Suddenly, I realize that of course he's been there! I've felt him, and others have commented on his presence there as well.

Do you see me there?

"Yes. I'm sorry I overlooked you in that place before."

Do you see her?

"Who?"

My Bride.

Suddenly, my blinders are removed, and I see all of the tables, not just the ones that have people from Fresh Wind at them. This place has become a safe haven for pastors from quite a number of churches. They come together and share their hearts, not only about their church problems but also about their own joys, struggles, and desires. They are blessing each other with time, prayer, support, and simply being together.

And there, right in the middle of all of this, is Jesus! *Right in the middle!* Talking with them, listening to them, planning and scheming with them, laughing with them, loving them. This is the Bride in her purest form.

"She's stunning. Look at how gracefully she moves. I have never seen her look more beautiful!"

She is beautiful. I love being close to her.

"What can we do?"

I want you, especially as leaders, to see the Bride as a whole. Don't use us/them language; work on including the entire Bride in all that you think and do. You've already seen this at work in your community when pastors pray together and share together. The moment they step over that threshold— the threshold of intimacy—the Bride begins to connect again. The parts of the Bride begin to move closer together, and she works together with all of her parts like she was always meant to be. You can see how beautiful she is when she is whole.

"What are you doing?"

I'm wooing my Bride. I'm drawing her back to me. I'm calling out to her scattered parts and drawing them back together. I'm weaving a new garment to replace the one that

was torn. This garment will cover all of my Bride. She will be glorious.

"I want to be part of that. I want to be woven into that fabric. I want to see your Bride in all of her beauty."

Then come closer.

Day 37

✠

What is the kingdom of God like?

Jesus gave considerable space in his messages to the Kingdom of God. Usually, he would use familiar analogies, called "parables," to describe some unfamiliar aspect of the Kingdom of God. His lessons were loaded with illustrations drawn from the disciples' culture. Do you remember any? For example, he spoke the language of farmers, referring to fields, seeds, weeds, and crops. He also spoke the language of fishermen, using images of nets and fish, wind and waves.

Today, begin by reading Matthew 13 as a primer. Then ask Jesus if he would show you his Kingdom by comparing it to something common in your world. But don't settle for the analogy—go for the conversation! Ask Jesus why his Kingdom is like that and why he chose to share that particular truth with you today. I suspect he'll choose something that is especially important to your own faith journey and your role in his Kingdom.

what is the kingdom of God like?

This question may be my absolute favorite. If I had only one question to ask, I would want to ask this one, because it promises to be so life-giving. The answer to this question opens up more of the world to my heart, and I can see again how intentional God has been with his Creation. I've got to find him!

"Father, will you join me?"

I'm here.

"Where will 'here' be today?"

Let's follow this path.

A beautiful little path winds ahead of us. I realize the path was made by the feet of those who have walked it before me. It's narrow, and the grass at its sides is attempting to grow over it. The air is sweet as we take to the path, and my heart is full.

"Will you open my eyes today, Father?"

What do you want to see?

"I want you to show me what your Kingdom is like."

He takes my hand, and we stroll along the path, just my Father and me.

My Kingdom is like a garden with many kinds of plants.

"I love your garden!"

I know that; you've seen my Kingdom there many times. But I want to show you even more today.

"Show me then."

We've come to a gate that straddles the path. I can see a garden within. I look to my Father, and he opens the gate with one hand and invites me in with the other.

My Kingdom is like a garden, and I am the Gardener. I plant all of the seeds in this beautiful garden, and I tend and care for the plants.

Over here, I have a flowerbed of annuals. They only have one season, but when they bloom, they are beautiful and fragrant. I enjoy all they contribute in their short lives.

We move on to another flowerbed.

This one has perennials. They endure and produce fruit over many years. They also have seasons, many of them, and with each one, they grow deeper and stronger roots. These plants have to endure many things, such as heat, rain, frost, and snow. And I have to prune them, too. I appreciate the endurance of these plants.

He points at the rest of the garden.

Look at the trees.

I see all kinds of fruit trees growing throughout the garden.

The fruit in my garden is sweet and good to eat. It feeds your heart and satisfies your longings. The fruit hangs down and

drops off when it is ripe, so those who rest beneath the trees can easily eat and be satisfied.

Some of my garden is planted carefully, creating designs out of the colors and textures of the plants. I've sown other areas of my Kingdom into a wild garden. The seeds were chosen carefully, but I scattered the seeds and allowed them to grow in whatever order and manner they chose. I love the mix of colors and the way they dance when the wind blows them.

I love my Garden Kingdom. I love what I see, what I smell, what I taste.

He finally tears his eyes away from the garden and smiles at me.

Will you stay here with me for a while?

"Yes!"

Day 38

✠

Show me your kingdom at work

We move now from Kingdom analogies to seeing the Kingdom at work in the world. If you feel up to asking God to show you, I think you'll be in for a treat.

Recently, I was at "Circle of Friends," a coffee house/worship time for people with disabilities. I sensed a strong presence of God the Father, so I asked him to show me his Kingdom. Immediately, I saw, with the eyes of my heart, that the entire room was like a giant champagne glass. He showed me many little acts of godly love that were "popping" like bubbles around the room. Kenny was hugging Amanda. Eddie was dancing to the Lord. Susan was giggling with Amber. Quenton was sniffing his care-worker's hair. And Chris was playing the harmonica with all his might. Soon, the "least of these" in our society (cf. Matthew 25) were overwhelming me with tears of love. I was seeing the Kingdom in action!

Now it's your turn! Are you ready? Then ask God to show his Kingdom to you.

show me your kingdom at work

I haven't left my spot with my Father in his Garden Kingdom. We have sat down under a beautiful tree. Just over from us, I can see butterflies fluttering above the plants and bees diving into flowers. There are so many things the gardener has just set into motion. I marvel at what he has created and continues to sustain.

"Father, will you show me your Kingdom at work?"

This is my Kingdom at work. Each member of Creation is doing what I have called it to do. Each member of Creation is contributing to the Garden Kingdom. The size of the creature doesn't make any difference. I have made each of them essential in my garden.

"Can you show me where you see this happening in my world?"

Circle of Friends.

Immediately, images flood my mind. I see faces crowding into my vision, wanting to be noticed. My heart smiles as I see these faces, because I know I've seen Jesus in them. These faces are so precious; they display the Kingdom in their eyes and share it with their smiles. These are our friends. The world calls them "disabled." I call them "gifted."

"Tell me more."

You've seen it. You've seen how they usher in the Kingdom, how I ride in on their praise. You've watched as they

have shared their gifts selflessly with one another. You've seen their tenderness toward those who are hurting and even received that tenderness yourself. You've seen their unbridled enthusiasm as they hear their favorite song and jump into singing and dancing. This is my Kingdom in its purest form.

The world sees them as pests, like bees or other insects in the garden. But I've put them in my garden for a reason. Contrary to what most people believe, they play an essential role in this garden I have designed.

You've seen this, too, but maybe not with open eyes. You've seen how they bring the Kingdom from one person to the next, how they brush by you and leave some of the Kingdom behind, how they deposit hope and life in your heart when they hug you, when they hold your hand, when they tell you you're their friend.

"I have seen it. It's absolutely marvelous!"

My Kingdom *is* marvelous. I've made it that way, but few get to experience it with my eyes. Viewing things from a human perspective is like using a microscope in the garden. There is so much happening that you overlook most of it, because you're dazzled by the colors. Your eyes are drawn to the bold and beautiful. But the Kingdom is just as real in the small things, the insignificant things that are easy to overlook.

"I know what you say is true. Can you help me to see your Kingdom in more of the little things? I don't want to overlook your Kingdom at *any* level. There's just too much that I would miss out on if I didn't see the world through your eyes. Lend me your eyes, Father!"

Day 39

✠

what kingdom works do you have for me today?

"Anyone who has faith in me will do what I have been doing. He will do even greater things than these, because I am going to the Father" (John 14:12).

The Kingdom of God is not to be merely understood or observed. You are invited to participate! Jesus Christ continues to act in this age, carrying out joint-ventures with people like you! We grow into the "greater things" as we are faithful in the little things (Luke 16: 10).

When I was in Mexico, I remember seeing a child being dropped off at an orphanage by his relatives. His father was long-gone, and his mother had just overdosed. As the little fellow bawled hysterically, we pled with the Lord, "What can we do? What does the Kingdom look like now?" God reminded us that some day he will wipe every tear from our eyes. He said to us, "Start now." That day, our Kingdom work was to apply tissue to a runny nose.

What will Kingdom work look like for you today?

what kingdom works do you have for me today?

In my heart, I see a medieval castle that is surrounded by high walls that protect not only the King but also all those who serve him within. I'm one of those people who make their home within the castle walls. But how do I serve him? What do I do within those walls?

Rather than just stumbling through my day and hoping my heart and actions are honoring to the King and his domain, I'm going to go directly to the King to ask what Kingdom works he has for me.

My King is not like any other. His castle and throne room are always open to me, and I can walk confidently into his presence at any time. When I do, I see him on his throne, but he doesn't sit there looking imposing and untouchable. Instead, he looks at me invitingly, as if to say, "Come and join me in my living room."

Today, I stand at the threshold of the throne room and take in what I see. My King beckons me to come close, and I race to his side. There's no cold indifference in his greeting and no hand extended to kiss a ring, just open arms to run into and a hug to receive.

I settle down at his feet and rest my head against his legs. His hand covers my head.

"King Jesus, what can I do in your Kingdom today?"

I'm so glad you asked rather than running ahead of me. My Kingdom is full of servants who don't ask me what I require

of them. Some of them have worked in the stables for years, but what I wanted of them was to be a sentry at my gates. Some have served as heralds and yet have never asked me for a message to announce. Others have elevated themselves to lofty heights in the eyes of the other servants, but they never come to my throne room. I have wonderful tasks to give to those who ask, tasks that bring life and hope to those who do them. Are you afraid of what I might ask you to do? Many are.

"I have no fear of that today. I only have to look back to what you've requested of me in the past and know that what you ask me to do today will be good. What Kingdom service can I do for you today?"

I want you to find a lost coin.

"A lost coin?"

Yes. Today, I want you to keep your eyes open for something that has been lost. The coin represents something that may seem trivial to others, but it matters to me, and I want it back!

"Who lost it?"

You did!

"Uh oh. Do you know where I might start to look for it?"

Yes. Start the search in your heart. Sweep the house clean, and you'll find it there. When you've found it, bring it to me, and we'll rejoice together.

"Why is this coin so important?"

Because I gave it to you, and I want you to have all that I have given. Every little gift that I give my servants is valuable. I don't give trinkets. The penny is not just a penny. It's a gift I've given, and I want you to enjoy it. Will you search for that coin today?

"Until I find it!"

Day 40

✠

Where should my focus be?

Throughout this forty-day conversation with God, we have moved back and forth from personal to public faith; from the realm of the heart into areas of social concern. We've done some inner purging and some outer working.

The questions we've covered should be revisited continually, but, as you can tell, there's no way to hold them all together at once. To this point, Eden and I have given the journey some direction, but now we hand those reins over to God. Your focus for each day must come from him lest you be spread too thin or experience guilt for failing to do it all.

So we'll begin today, as you'll begin again and again from this point forward, with this question: "Lord, where should my focus be today? What's your agenda? What do you want me to ask today?" Rather than providing a cookie-cutter outline for your regular prayer life, we hope that through reading this book, you've learned and experienced enough to enter into lively discussions with your living and very best Friend.

where should my focus be?

There are so many things in this world to distract me. Most of these distractions I could defend as "good things," because I'm doing them in or for the church. Many times I have been carried away completely with what I was doing and forgotten for whom I was doing it. But I want to be more intentional in my "doings," and the only way I know how to do that is to ask my Father where he wants my focus to be.

"Father, I need help."

He comes to me in my heart's yard. I stand surveying his work and grin at the progress.

"You've *really* started something now, Father."

I know, and I like what I see! And I have plans to do so much more.

"That's great. But where do you want me to focus today? What do you want my eyes to behold?"

I want you to behold this.

He captures my face in his hands and turns it to his. His eyes look into mine, and I drink in all that they pour out onto me—love, mercy, compassion, and grace, intimacy and friendship, joy and peace that surpasses all understanding. His eyes have become a fountain that gushes over me, soaking me with living water. I stand dripping in my heart's yard, thoroughly soaked, and thoroughly refreshed.

"I don't want to look anywhere else, Father."

Good! There's so much I can teach you when you focus on my eyes. There's so much I can pour out onto you when your eyes stay on me. There's so much you can do when your gaze never leaves mine.

"How do I keep this focus? How will I be able to avoid getting distracted?"

I'll teach you to dance. You'll learn to move gracefully with me, following my lead, and you'll never have to look at your feet. You'll learn to trust me completely, even when you are unfamiliar with the dance. We'll hear the same music, follow the same beat, and dance like long-time partners. You will allow me to lead, not wrestling your will against mine. We will dance our way through this life. We'll dance a waltz, celebrate with a jig, and stomp our feet in a war dance. All of this will be accomplished while you focus on me. There will be no time to be distracted; distraction will have no power over you!

My heart is pounding. I'm a little scared—and excited. I've been invited to dance through this life with my Father. But I'm not a good dancer, and if I were to describe my moves on the dance floor, "graceful" would not be on the list. Can I really dance? Can I really dance with him?

You're focusing on your feet Eden. Look in my eyes.

I lift my eyes from my feet to look into my Father's face. All at once, the life in his eyes settles down my insecurities.

"When do my lessons begin?"

Right now! Let's start with a waltz.

afterword

How did it go? I trust that throughout this exercise, God has opened your eyes and ears to some powerful truths, both through Eden and I and directly in your own heart.

Many of the questions we asked God can be revisited frequently. But perhaps by now you've composed your own array of creative questions. If so, by all means, submit them by e-mail to info@freshwindpress.com.

Here are some favorites for further prayer that we didn't include in this book:

• God, when I meet you at heaven's gate, how will you greet me? What will you do? What will you say?

• God, in what Bible story would you like to meet me? Do I remind you of one of the characters in that story? How does this story tie into my life?

• God, if there were any sight on earth that you could show me, what would it be? May I see it now?

• God, if you could play a game with me, what would it be? Why?

• God, do you have a term of endearment or nickname for me? What does it mean?

• Lord, is there a wonderful memory in my life where you'd like to meet me? Where were you then? What were you doing?

• Lord, is there a painful memory in my life where you'd like to meet me? Where were you then? What were you doing? What do you want to show or tell me there? How will you redeem this?

• Lord, how would you have me pray for my family? How do you see my parents? My siblings? My spouse? My children? What part of their destiny would you have me fight for in prayer?

• Lord, where are the front lines of Kingdom warfare? What weapons have you given me? What part have you given me to play?

• Lord, what spiritual gifts and ministries have you given me? Where and how can I put them to use?

• Lord, would you lead me to some godly mentors? What do you want me to learn? Who should I be mentoring? What can I share?

• Lord, what book or chapter of the Bible should I be meditating on these days? What themes do you want me to notice? Where does this address my life situation? How shall I respond?

As you can see, the interactions you can have with God are virtually endless. I pray that is exactly what you will have: an eternal conversation with your Lord. May the Spirit of Christ quicken your heart to hear his voice and see his face, all to the glory of God.

thanks from eden

To those who pondered my journal and then encouraged me to write. You were the first to see what Jesus was planning.

To the many intercessors who prayed specifically for me while I wrote. You paved the way for me each day, making a way that I couldn't find alone.

To those who believed in my heart and fanned the flame: Lorie and Jodi. If this book was a baby, then you were my midwives. You have treasured what was growing inside me and have helped to nurture it to life. Thanks for rejoicing with me over every question asked and every answer heard.

To Justice and Dominic, who would wake up and greet me with a warm hug and kiss every morning just as I was done my writing. It made getting up worth it!

To Stephen, who had to endure the clicking of the computer keys just outside his bedroom door early each morning and is still able to tell me he loves me.

To Brad, who invited me on this journey without knowing if I could see it through. [*Brad - "Yes I did."*] You put more faith in my abilities than I ever could. I love you.

To Kevin Miller, our brilliant editor, and his lovely wife Heidi, who juggled proof-reading into her already full schedule.

And finally, to my Mom and Dad, for blessing my name-change.

also available from fresh wind press

Can You Hear Me? Tuning In to the God Who Speaks
By Brad Jersak   ISBN 0-9733586-0-2

A compelling collection of biblical and historical research, real life experiences, and inspiring exercises on listening prayer. God desires to transform your prayer times into intimate conversations, real meetings with a Living Friend. In this book, you will learn that encountering God is simpler and more interactive than you ever dreamed. **Study guide also available**.

Children Can You Hear Me? How to Hear and See God
By Brad Jersak   ISBN 0-9733586-1-0

God longs to open the eyes and ears of faith in every boy and girl— even the child in you. This hardcover picture book features full color illustrations by Ken Save and a chapter from _Can You Hear Me?_ that teaches adults how to nurture children into a lifestyle of listening prayer.

Available online at www.freshwindpress.com
or at your local Christian bookstore